PERFECT PHRASES™
for
SETTING
PERFORMANCE
GOALS

PERFECT PHRASES™

for

SETTING PERFORMANCE GOALS

second edition

**Hundreds of Ready-to-Use Phrases for
Communicating Any Performance Plan or Review**

Robert Bacal and Douglas Max

New York   Chicago   San Francisco   Lisbon   London   Madrid   Mexico City
Milan   New Delhi   San Juan   Seoul   Singapore   Sydney   Toronto

ISBN   978-0-07-174505-5
MHID   0-07-174505-X

Library of Congress Cataloging -in-Publication Data
Bacal, Robert.
    Perfect Phrases for setting performance goals / by Robert Bacal, Douglas Max
    — 2nd ed.
      p. cm.
    ISBN 978-0-07-174505-5 (alk. paper)
    1. Employees—Rating of. 2. Employees—Rating of—Terminology
  3. Personnel management. I. Max, Douglas. II. Title

    HF5549.5.R3M2583 2011
    658.3'125—dc22

                                                        2010038168

This is a *CWL Publishing Enterprises Book* produced for McGraw-Hill by CWL Publishing Enterprises, Inc., Madison, Wisconsin, www.cwlpub.com.

McGraw-Hill books are available at special quantity discounts to use as premiums and sales promotions or for use in corporate training programs. To contact a representative, please e-mail us at bulksales@mcgraw-hill.com.

This book is printed on acid-free paper.

Contents

Contents

PART TWO. PERFECT PHRASES FOR SETTING PERFORMANCE GOALS

Contents

Section Two. Performance Goals for General Management Responsibilities

Contents

Contents

Contents

Contents

Contents

Contents

Preface to the Second Edition

There's a popular misconception that the work of improving performance starts and ends with the performance appraisal meeting. If you look at what most managers do, it seems like they believe this misconception. The time they spend in performance appraisals is just about all the time they spend on improving performance. As a result, the many benefits of managing performance are lost as they focus solely on the appraisal process, the end point and, unfortunately, the wrong point.

Is there a secret to improving work performance? In a way. It's simple. The secret for organizations, managers, and employees is to put more emphasis on making sure managers and employees know what they must accomplish. When each employee understands what he or she needs to do to succeed, it's much easier for that person to contribute. It's also much easier for managers to do their jobs, improve productivity, and manage proactively. Otherwise, managers will spend far too much time stomping out many, many small fires rather than preventing them.

Preface to the Second Edition

Clear purpose helps everyone succeed, and that's what everyone wants and benefits from. Appraisals look in the rear view mirror and involve looking at things that are often too late to change. Planning performance—setting goals and objectives—is the opposite. It's looking forward to deal with things that are yet to come and are still under our control.

This book helps you set performance goals and objectives—those statements that are used to aim and guide performance throughout the year. These same performance goals are also used to evaluate employee performance and, more importantly, identify barriers to performance so they can be removed. The purpose of this book is to make the goal-setting process as easy and painless as possible. When you get the goals in place, it also makes the appraisal process much easier. It's the *goals* that make employee reviews and appraisals work!

The performance goals ("perfect phrases") offered in this book should help you and your employees come to agreement about what is expected of employees (and their managers) to maximize the value each adds to the organization.

These phrases, translated into goals and objectives for your employees, will improve your ability to track progress all year long and reduce the stress and anxiety often associated with performance reviews when the review criteria are fuzzy, vague, and misunderstood.

Before you start, one thing. Please read the introductory material. It explains some important issues regarding objectivity and specificity of goals and objectives. We believe that for most employees and managers, what is most important is that the "goals in use" are negotiated and based on a mutual, common understanding of the meaning of the words. We stress a negotiated common understanding approach because it's virtually impossible to set precise, specific unambiguous goals for many jobs while keeping the goals relevant and meaningful. If you skip the front material you will miss important parts that make the rest of this book make sense.

If you would like more in-depth coverage and explanations of performance management and performance review processes, try the following:

- *The Busy Learner's Kit for Making Performance Management and Appraisal VALUABLE*, by Robert Bacal, CreateSpace, 2010
- *Manager's Guide to Performance Reviews*, by Robert Bacal, McGraw-Hill, 2003
- *Performance Management*, by Robert Bacal, McGraw-Hill, 1999

If you need assistance with writing performance reviews, try the first book in the Perfect Phrases series:

- *Perfect Phrases for Performance Reviews, Second Edition*, by Douglas Max and Robert Bacal, McGraw-Hill, 2010

We'd also like to invite you to make use of The Performance Management Resource Center on the Internet. You'll find hundreds of articles and tips on the performance management process and be able to interact with others involved in performance management. You will also find some useful job aids connected with performance improvement, including our Helpcard series for busy learners. You can access these materials at www.performance-appraisals.org.

Acknowledgments

You'd think that writing books like this is easy. It's harder than it looks. We'd like to thank John Woods of CWL Publishing Enterprises and McGraw-Hill for their patience, perseverance, and contributions to this book.

Finally, a special thanks is due to Nancy Moore, who contributed to a number of the sections in this book with both general and specific ideas on goals and works with me on all my books.

—Robert Bacal

Part One

Background for Developing and Writing Performance Goals

Using This Book to Write Better Performance Goals

Before we start you on the path to writing better performance goals, and before we explain how to use this book to help improve both individual work performance and overall performance of your work unit or company, we need to place performance goals within the business and management context and examine why it's important to take the time to establish performance goals for employees.

No. Scratch that. *Important* isn't the right word. Crucial, critical, and essential are better. If you want better employee performance, engaged staff, higher productivity, and, believe it or not, better morale, you MUST have employees who understand what constitutes their jobs, what they need to achieve, and the levels of achievement needed. Goals and objectives do all that.

Wait, we're jumping ahead.

After all, if you don't see the sense or value in working with employees to set goals, it's not likely you're going to do it.

What Are Performance Goals Used For?

There's a popular misconception that the way to improve performance, whether on an individual basis or for a work unit, is to appraise and evaluate it after the fact. You're probably familiar with the performance appraisal process that is often used once a year. You know the one. It's the time of the year where managers and employees would rather crawl across cut glass than meet to do the appraisals.

Eventually, if nagged enough, manager and employee sit down to discuss and evaluate performance for the past year, or at least the employee's performance. Forms are used to record the conversation and convince everyone that something valuable is going on. They don't convince anyone.

Sometimes the process goes smoothly and sometimes not. More often than not, the appraisal meetings do little to meet the needs of employee or manager, and neither considers them helpful. Or worse, they dread them. Mostly they dread them.

The performance appraisal can be valuable, but not as a stand-alone process. In fact, the many benefits of managing and appraising performance are lost when managers focus solely on the appraisal process as the end point. It's like driving while looking in the rearview mirror: you see what's already past and beyond your control.

If we want to improve performance, we need a forward-looking process to *prevent* performance problems. We need a forward-looking process to harness and coordinate the work of individual employees so we increase the effectiveness of the work unit and the company in general. After all, that's what we really want—for each employee to contribute to the effectiveness of the whole and, to whatever extent possible, to have everyone win: the manager, the work unit and company, and, most of all, the employee. When the performance management is used to help the employee "win," everyone ends up winning.

The secret of success—for organizations, managers, and employees—is to put more emphasis on making sure employees and managers know what needs to be accomplished in the present and future. When an employee understands what he or she needs to do to succeed, it's much easier to contribute. It's also much easier for managers to do their jobs, to improve productivity, and to manage proactively, rather than spend time stamping out small fires after the fact. Clear purpose helps everyone succeed, and, bottom line, that's what we all want.

Enter performance goals. Like the bull's-eye on an archery target, performance goals specify what the employee needs to aim at. Let's look at how they can help.

For the Organization

To succeed, organizations need to be able to coordinate the work of individual employees and work units, so that everyone is pulling in the same direction. Performance goals provide the foundation to allow this kind of coordination to occur.

The process of setting individual performance goals provides the mechanism for translating the goals of the organization as a whole into smaller chunks that are then assigned or delegated to individual employees. That's necessary because organizations achieve their overall goals to the extent that each employee does his or her part in completing the right job tasks in effective ways.

For the Manager

It's easy to think about performance management and goal setting as "overhead." In a world where many managers are exceedingly busy, there's a tendency to think that performance management and goal setting are ways to create more worth-less paper that has little to do with the manager's success.

That's not true. Yes, the process takes time and effort. What's easy to miss is that goal setting is an investment that pays off through higher productivity. Let's look at how properly set goals help managers.

First, most managers want employees to do their jobs with a minimum of direct supervision. Employees who require constant guidance and direction eat up a lot of managerial time, not to mention patience. Where do performance goals fit?

When an employee knows what he or she needs to accomplish and what is expected, it's a lot easier for that employee to work with minimal supervision. Also, helping employees understand how their individual work contributes to the overall goals of the organization enables them to make better decisions on how to spend their time so that their work is consistent with the priorities of the organization.

The result? Employees know what they must do, how well they must do it, and why they are doing it. That means there's much less need for ongoing supervision. Also, clear performance goals allow managers to empower their staff to make decisions relevant to their work without having to consult the manager on every little question. For those of you who are believers in the "employee engagement movement" you'll also recognize that clear goals, through creating empowered employees, encourage employees to find meaning in their work and increase their engagement.

Second, clear goals allow employees to monitor their own progress year-round and correct their efforts as necessary. If employees know what they need to accomplish, they can look at their results as they go and identify barriers to achieving those goals AT THE TIME. Once again, this ability to self-monitor and self-correct means less managerial time is needed to supervise and guide employees.

Third, the performance appraisal/review becomes much easier, causes far less anxiety, and goes much faster when there are clear performance goals. In fact, the better the performance goals, the clearer they are, and the more measurable they are, the less managers and employees have to venture into the realm of vague opinions about performance during the appraisal process. Combine this with the fact that performance goals allow employees to monitor both their efforts and results throughout the year and we get an appraisal process that is much more effective and yields no surprises for the employee.

Finally, let's consider the value of performance goals in helping to proactively identify barriers to performance. It does little good to identify poor performance after the fact or after it has affected the organization. Clear performance goals make it much easier to monitor performance throughout the year and catch situations where performance may be veering off course. What follows is a diagnostic process in which employee and manager can figure out what might be causing performance deficits and take action early. In other words, the goals serve as the basis for an "early warning system," because they are specific enough to allow employee and manager to gauge progress all year long.

For the Employee

Most employees want and need to know four things about their work so they can contribute and feel comfortable about where they are in the organization:

- What do I need to accomplish?
- Why am I doing what I'm doing?
- How well must I do it?
- How am I doing?

Job descriptions are of some help in outlining what an employee needs to accomplish, but they usually don't specify the "how well" part. They are often out of date. Performance appraisals can provide information about how an employee is doing, but they are usually not done often enough to provide enough information.

Ideally, performance goals specify what employees need to do and how well the work should be done. They are more specific than job descriptions and are based on what an employee actually does, not on what the job description says the employee does. This helps the employee have a better understanding of his or her job. That's always a good thing. The more an employee understands the job, the more likely he or she can contribute.

Of course, employees want to know how they are doing. As we mentioned earlier regarding the organization and the manager, clear performance goals help employees to monitor their efforts and assess their results during the year and provide a basis for performance appraisals and reviews. The goals can also serve as a basis for ongoing discussion between manager and employee or, for that matter, among employees, aimed at improving work contributions. Employees can receive recognition for accomplishments throughout the year, since it's easy to identify when an employee has met or exceeded a performance goal.

The bottom line here is that performance goals help employees know where they need to go and what they need to do to get there, and they help them determine how they're doing.

Where Do Performance Goals Come From?

Performance goals don't appear out of the blue, and they aren't created from nothing. Where do they come from?

Since performance goals are used to coordinate and aim employees so they can contribute to organizational perform-ance, they need to link to the goals of the organization. Perfor-mance goals can't result in better performance unless they are derived from the goals and priorities of the work unit and the company. We recommend that performance goals be based upon the needs of the organization. That's where they must orig-inate to be most effective. (In the next chapter, we'll map out the sequence that links individual goals to organizational goals.)

It's not uncommon for managers to pull or generate per-formance goals from job descriptions. That's not a good idea.

Job descriptions are notorious for being out of date and far too general to provide meaningful yearly goals for employees. Also, they do not take into account the individual strengths and weaknesses of any particular employee, since they don't describe people, but positions. Job descriptions may be useful as back-ground material for setting goals, but keep in mind that it's quite possible, and even desirable, for different people in the same posi-tion, with the same job description, to have different goals that take into account their unique strengths and capabilities.

Finally, individual performance goals develop from corpo-rate goals through discussion and dialogue between the man-ager and each employee. The goals are set and negotiated individually and collaboratively. They are not imposed, dictated, or "given" to the employee. Why? Here are the main reasons:

1. Most employees—those who have been in their positions for a while—know how they can best contribute. They know

their jobs and how well they need to do them. Employees are in the best positions to set their own goals.

2. Since we want employees to buy into the goals and treat them as relevant and important, they need to participate in developing the goals that apply to them. When people are active participants in setting goals, they tend to work harder to achieve them, since they have a feeling of ownership.

3. Performance goals, by themselves, are important, but so are the discussions that generate them. As you will see later, the discussion between manager and employee serves many purposes, the least of which involves writing down goals. The discussion helps employees understand where they fit in the organization and provides meaning and context for their work. It helps employees understand the importance and larger purpose of their work. We know that when employees feel their work has meaning, they tend to be much more motivated and diligent in their efforts to achieve those goals.

So, to summarize, performance goals are based on the needs of the organization and are generated through discussion and dialogue with employees. If you skip or gloss over the dialogue, the process becomes less meaningful and more a paper chase.

How to Use This Book

Developing performance goals isn't easy. It requires an investment of time and effort by the manager and each employee. The purpose of this book is to make the process a bit shorter, less frustrating, and easier for all parties.

The book is organized into two parts. The first part is this one. READ IT! Don't simply assume that you know what's in the first part, since it's absolutely critical that you understand the details of performance goals and goal setting. We'll provide those to you and map out how to go about setting goals so they work and how to go about using the goals you've set.

Once you've read this first part, you'll be ready to make use of the goal phrases in this book. You can use it in several ways.

First, you can use the statements in this book "as is," to the extent that they fit your situation. We've tried to generate goal phrases that will fit a wide variety of jobs and job responsibilities, and we've categorized them to make them easy to find. However, you must make sure that the goals you use reflect your situation; your company; and the needs of company, management, and employee. That means you may need to customize extensively.

Second, you may find that one of the strengths of this book is that it can stimulate employee and management thinking about goal setting. These phrases provide good starting points for reflection and discussion. Just keep in mind the point—performance improvement and coordination.

Generally, it's a good idea to read relevant parts of this book prior to sitting down with employees to set goals. Before meeting with each employee, take a few minutes to go through the sections you think are relevant to him or her, and take note or jot down any goals you think may be applicable.

Consider sharing the book with employees beforehand. To reduce the time you spend in goal-setting meetings, provide a copy of this book to the employee and ask him or her to go through and identify a certain number of goals—let's say, 10–15—that might fit his or her job. This will work only if the employee understands the job well and also understands where your work unit and company are going in the next year, so consider spending a few minutes with the employee before the goal-setting meeting to discuss those issues.

What's Next?

Now that we've covered some of the basics, we'll guide you step by step through the goal-setting process and provide you with valuable suggestions for ensuring that everyone benefits from the investment in goal setting. As you go through the book, remember this: Every minute you spend in setting proper goals and objectives with your employees is going to be returned to you over and over throughout the year by removing the need for strict supervision, increased employee engagement, and reducing the time you spend during performance appraisals. Goal setting saves time. Invest in it!

Setting Performance Goals That Work

What are performance goals? Different people use different terminology, like performance objectives, or standards of performance, which have slightly differing meanings but have in common some central aspects. All of these describe what an employee needs to achieve in order to contribute to the overall success of his or her organization. Usually the statements describe the results an employee is to create rather than specify how the result is to be obtained, but there are numerous exceptions to this rule. If an employee achieves the goals or exceeds them, he or she is doing well. If not, then it's important to discover why the shortfall occurred and take remedial action.

Specific and Measurable Goals?
A Balancing Act

Despite the rhetoric of "experts" there is no one "right" format for performance goals except to observe this:

The right format for performance goals is that which allows you to coordinate employee work, improve productivity and effectiveness, and reduce misunderstandings about what is expected.

There are formats and ways of writing goals so they tend to be more useful, but wording performance goals is often a balancing act. Ideally, performance goals should be as specific as possible. The more specific a goal is, the more likely the employee and the manager will have a common, shared understanding about what it means. That's important.

An example might help. Consider this phrasing: "Ensure that all work is done properly." This is an example of an exceedingly vague goal. It will most certainly mean different things to different people. When the time comes to discuss or evaluate progress toward the achievement of this goal, these differences in understanding will cause conflict. This goal is simply too general.

Contrast this with a more specific goal: "Complete monthly financial reports and submit to manager by the end of each month." This one is far more specific and less likely to be interpreted in different ways. When it comes time to determine if the employee has achieved this goal, the process is fairly straightforward. All the manager and the employee have to do is answer the question, "Were the monthly reports completed and submitted to the manager by the end of each month?"

We want specific goals, and we want goals that can also be measured, if possible. With our vague example, there's no measurement criterion we can apply to determine if the goal has been met. The second includes a criterion: we can measure whether the employee achieved the goal if we check whether the report was submitted by the end of each month. Or can we? Here's the catch—the balancing act, if you want to call it that. The more specific the objective, the narrower it is. Narrow goals don't cover much ground because they are so specific. Therefore, the more specific and narrow the goals, the more goals you need to accurately describe what an employee needs to accomplish and the more work is involved in both writing the goals and measuring goal achievement.

At some point you hit the point of diminishing returns, where setting goals becomes so time-consuming and frustrating that the goal-setting process costs more than it benefits. Similarly there is a real cost involved in actual measurement of goal achievement, particularly in cases where the "indicators" are not tracked already. For example, it's easy to track sales as a criterion because it's already recorded, but it may be tougher to measure customer retention in a retail environment, because that's not data that is routinely recorded. Also, in the pursuit of specificity and measurability, we can end up with goal statements that are very long and involved. For example, take a look at this goal statement:

> *Complete monthly financial statements containing final revenue and cost figures, broken down by capital expenditures and salary categories, accurate and not needing revision after submission, and received by the manager by month's end, and to the satisfaction of the manager.*

It's specific, right? It can be measured. But can you imagine writing dozens of these for each employee? It's a problem. Most effective managers try to attain some level of balance, so that the goals set are detailed enough to ensure that employee and manager share a common understanding of the meaning of the goals but not so detailed that the goals take hours and hours to craft.

You need to be aware of another "gotcha" when writing specific and measurable goals. As you write more specific and measurable goals, you may find that the goals are less and less important to the employee's actual contributions to the organization. In the pursuit of the easily measurable, it's possible to end up with a set of goals that are so picky and niggling that they are really irrelevant and, therefore, useless. *That's because it's easy to measure trivial and unimportant things in objective, observable ways, but it's hard to measure important things.*

Where does that leave us? We still want to phrase goals so they are as measurable and specific as possible, but we have to balance that desire with practical workplace issues, as we've described above. This balancing act becomes a lot less important if you take the position that one function of setting performance goals is to develop a common understanding between manager and employee. If the dialogue and communication between the parties is effective, then the goals need not be quite as specific as would otherwise be the case. That's one reason why it's so important that the goal-setting process involve both employee and manager as active participants.

In any event, we'll take the position that you are going to use your common sense during goal setting. Make the goals as specific as you need them to be to improve performance.

The Objectivity Bugaboo—Holy Grail of Goals

If you read about goal and objective setting in the workplace or in education, you will often come across the admonition that goals and objectives should be . . . well, objective. That's in the sense of being the opposite of subjective but often we don't think about what that means, or whether that is even possible. In human "affairs" is it possible to eliminate subjective judgments, biases, and errors? Should we strive to do so with employee goals? There's no pat answer to the latter, but there is one for the former question. It is NOT possible to eliminate subjectivity, bias, and error even in measuring something that you would think could be determined objectively and absolutely.

Consider a simple example—your height and weight. What is your true height or your true weight down to three decimal points? One person measures you at five foot five and .345 of an inch (5.345) while someone else measures you and gets 5.320. You *will* get this when you look for exactitude and precision. The more objective and precise you want your measurements, the more you will start to see that your measurements are not perfect, accurate, *or* objective.

Our systems to set goals and objectives don't generally expose this weakness in how we interact in the world, so we come to believe that it is possible to create goals that are absolute, reliably and objectively measurable, and meaningful. It's not. Again, it's all relative. You can create goals that can be more or less objective, but you can't create goals that can be absolutely free of subjectivity, bias, and error.

That is why you strive for agreement and mutual understanding, rather than searching for that which, while fascinating us, does not exist. Objectivity is the holy grail of goal setting.

On the second issue, whether one can argue it's good to have only objective criteria (well, relatively objective), you'll have to decide the proper mix for yourself. Keep in mind that judgments are subjective and open to interpretation, and humans make thousands of judgments each day. Provided we take a negotiated cooperative approach to both goal setting and determining goal attainment, the issue is irrelevant. Just remember that objectivity is relative.

Where Does That Leave SMART Goals?

You may be familiar with the most common "formula" for establishing goals and objectives for both performance and learning—SMART. It's somewhat amusing to find out that this well-used acronym has so many different meanings:

S – specific, significant, stretching
M – measurable, meaningful, motivational
A – agreed upon, attainable, achievable, action-oriented, acceptable
R – realistic, relevant, reasonable, rewarding, results-oriented
T – time-based, timely, tangible, trackable

If you're counting, the various combinations yield at least 900 different specific meanings of the SMART acronym.

SMART goals should be seen as a target to aim at, while keeping in mind that your business and management needs should drive the format and style of the goals and objectives you create. Remember the ultimate guiding principle: goals are a means of expressing mutual and shared meaning about what the employee is expected to achieve.

As indicated earlier, we want measurable results-oriented goals because we want accountability, and we want clarity.

That said, understand that we aren't talking about absolutes when we talk about SMART goals and objectives. For example, specificity is relative, not absolute. There is no point at which one can arbitrarily say *this* is specific and this is not. It's almost always the case that a goal can be made more specific or less so. The real question is: Is this goal specific enough to guide the employee's performance while minimizing the hassle of creating and measuring the goal? Is it specific *enough* for the purpose?

This conflicts somewhat with the "expert" advice of those that present the SMART acronym as an absolute. It's not. Only you and the employee can determine how specific a goal need be, what constitutes meaningfulness, or how results-oriented the goal should be. You and your employees are paid to "use your head." Do that! It's impossible to give you a "cookbook" approach you can apply mindlessly.

Parts of a Goal Statement

A goal statement has two major parts. The first describes what the employee must accomplish, the "what." The second part describes the criteria that will be applied to determine if the employee has achieved the "what." Let's look at some examples.

Consider this statement: "Reduce overall spending by 10%." The first part—"reduce overall spending"—describes the "what." The second part—"by 10%"—describes the metric that can be used to determine if the overall goal is achieved. By itself, the first part is too vague. By adding the second part, the criterion, we now have a more specific and concrete way of determining success and evaluating progress toward the goal throughout the year. Is it specific enough? You decide. You could make it more specific by adding more. For example, you could say, "Reduce overall spending by 10% while keeping customer complaints at current level." You could make it even more specific, infinitely. Ultimately what is "enough" depends on what you require to create common understanding.

Not all goals are so easily quantified. Take this example: "Prepare accounting statements that are approved without significant modification by the independent auditors." In this case, the "what" is "prepare accounting statements." The criterion, however, is not something that is counted or measured. If the accounting statements are approved "without significant modification" by the auditors, then the employee has achieved this goal. (Of course, it would be good if you could define or describe what you mean by "significant.") This makes perfect sense. This goal accurately reflects the business importance of having auditors provide the stamp of approval. So criteria can be quantifiable ("by 10%") or simply demonstrable ("approved . . . by the independent auditors").

Sometimes, goals may reference criteria that already exist and need not be repeated in the goal itself. Here's an example: "Prepare annual budgets in accordance with the guidelines provided by the chief financial officer." In this case, we don't need to list all the particulars contained in the guidelines. It's enough to refer to them more generally; this can save time.

There's another way to specify the performance criteria. In the examples above, we've focused on what we want (10% reduction, approval by auditors, conformance to guidelines). Sometimes it's easier to specify an absence of what we don't want. For example, "Receive no more than three validated customer complaints per year" or "Assemble 100 widgets per month with no more than one widget requiring rework."

Goals Without Criteria

There's no doubt that performance goals that are clear and specify measurement criteria are generally more useful than those that don't. Does that mean you can specify only goals that have criteria? Also, is it OK to have fuzzy, opinion-based criteria?

There are some situations where it may make sense to set performance goals without criteria or with very fuzzy, subjective criteria. Some contributions are simply not easily quantifiable or even observable in the specifics without the task of setting goals becoming more than it's worth.

Consider the issue of contributions to a work team. It's possible to write a number of specific goals for this domain. For example, "Contribute at least one idea per meeting" or "Communicate well in teams as measured by his or her team members' surveys." In some situations, those specifics strengthen the goals; in other situations, they might interfere with getting work done or create unnecessary work. Do we really want to have someone count who comes up with what ideas at a staff meeting?

Let's consider another example, from goals for support staff: "Prioritize phone calls to the satisfaction of the manager." Maybe, depending on your situation, you could set a criterion that is more specific and less subjective, based on the priorities of the manager. That would strengthen the goal, but it might make more sense to make a list of priorities to post for support staff as a guide, rather than to write a goal that is long and complicated.

Perhaps we need to ask ourselves two questions. Is it worthwhile to list a number of specific goals that are measurable and observable? Are we really going to use those criteria anyway?

You have to make your own judgments about what you need, but it may be sufficient in some cases to have a general goal that serves as a reminder to employees that, for example, teamwork is important. When we simply want to point out the importance of something, rather than actually measure that something, general goals can suffice as the "aiming" device.

One final comment about goals and criteria: you get what you measure. Before you develop a measure of performance, think through the consequences of evaluating performance in that way. Make sure that the results are what you want. Some measures may lead to clashes among goals for an employee or to conflicts among employees. In such cases, setting performance goals could hurt performance by undermining collaboration and negatively affecting productivity in the work unit.

The Goal-Setting Process

Here are the basic steps in setting goals with an employee.

1. Preparation and Prework

Several weeks in advance, the manager explains the goal-setting process, its purpose, and its benefits. Prior to the goal-setting meeting, the manager and the employee review the goals of the work unit and the organization and identify what the employee might do to contribute to achieving them. Experienced employees can often generate goals beforehand for discussion at the meeting.

2. The Meeting

The manager explains the purpose of the meeting, reiterating the basic purposes of the process. Then, he or she outlines the work-unit goals. Sometimes the manager and the employee review the job description and update it to reflect any changes in responsibilities or job activities. The manager plays a facilitating role—encouraging the employee to define critical work activities, goals, and criteria, rather than telling the employee what he or she needs to achieve. The two develop a set of goals together. Discuss the relative priorities of the various goals, as well. Once a list is done, it's also good to discuss whatever the employee needs in order to achieve the goals (help from the manager, new tools, extra resources).

3. Action Planning and Follow-Up

Some goals may be sufficiently complex that they require formal action plans, with progress indicators, timelines, and action steps. If so, the employee should develop action plans and then review them with the manager within a few weeks of the goal-setting meeting.

Follow-up involves ongoing communication about progress made or not made toward achieving the goals. Although it's technically not a part of goal setting, follow-up is an absolute necessity to make the whole process work and justify the time spent creating goals.

Ten Tips for Setting Performance Goals

1. Individualize performance goals for each employee, even if there are a number of employees with identical job descriptions. Employees with the same job titles and descriptions rarely do exactly the same things and can contribute in ways different from their peers, provided their unique needs, skills, and abilities are recognized in their performance goals and they are encouraged to use their strengths.

2. The goal setting process is probably more important than the goals created. It's the dialogue between manager and employee that develops an employee's sense of his or her contributions to the organization as a whole. Goal setting is about communication, as is the whole performance management process.

3. It's easy to write performance goals that are measurable, but it's hard to write goals that are measurable and meaningful or important. Don't shy away from areas that are hard to measure if they are important to the organization.

4. Technically perfect goals are great, but it's more important that the employee and the manager share the same understanding of what each goal means and how it links to the success of the organization.

5. Even goals that are phrased perfectly are useless unless there is communication about those goals throughout the year. Two major reasons for having goals are to allow employees to monitor themselves during the year and to form the basis for formal and/or informal discussions during the year to identify and remove any barriers to achieving the goals.

6. The process of setting individual performance goals should take place after the employee's work unit has its set of goals for the year. Then each employee's goals can be directly tied to what the work unit needs to accomplish. That's the ideal situation. If that's not possible in your company it's still important to go through the goal setting process.

7. Performance goals should specify the results the employee is expected to achieve rather than how the results are to be achieved. We don't want to be too rigid about this, since means and ends are not so black and white. In situations where the process to be followed is as important as the result, it should be mentioned (e.g., "File statutory information in accordance with government requirements"). Often process-based goals (means) can be turned into results (ends), so let's focus on common understanding and flexibility.

8. Shift your thinking about performance goals from using goals to evaluate performance to using goals to aim and guide performance. Proper aiming and guiding means you need to evaluate less.

9. It's possible to generate dozens, sometimes hundreds of goals for any one employee. Clearly the cost and effort of doing so can outweigh the benefits. Strive to cover the important functions. Try to limit the number of goals for any employee to 10 or so, with those goals covering at least 80% of what the employee actually does.

10. Goals should not be etched in stone. The work world is fast-paced and changes often. It's not uncommon for managers at any level to modify or even completely remove some goals during the year. Priorities change. Keep in mind that as the goals of the work unit are shuffled, you and your employees may need to modify some individual performance goals or reallocate them to other employees.

Getting the Most from Performance Goals

We've walked you through the basic process of set-ting performance goals. Keep in mind that perform-ance goals are tools to improve and manage performance. Like any tool, they do no good if they're left in the back of the drawer to gather dust. You can buy a hammer, but unless you know how to use it, and then you use it effectively, it's not going to be of much good.

The last chapter ended with 10 hints important for setting and using performance goals. In this chapter we're going to pro-vide you with essential tips and guidelines to make sure you get maximum benefits from the goals you set with your employees.

Using the Goals During the Year

Setting goals is only the first step in maximizing performance. You need to use those goals during the year as tools to manage and improve performance. Here are some important tips and guidelines.

1. *Ensure that there is adequate communication about perform-ance goals between you and each employee during the year.* Performance goals aren't "fire and forget" tools. They bring

about maximum productivity when they are coupled with a communication process that goes on all year.

2. *Consider a regular and scheduled way to communicate about progress toward the goals.*

   One way to communicate about goals and progress toward those goals is to have some regular and formalized way to do so. There are a number of ways, including the following:

   a. Set up a regular reporting system in which employees submit a brief statement (let's say monthly or quarterly) outlining "where they are" in terms of hitting their goals. Not only does this help you know what is going on, but it also makes the performance goals more visible to each employee and emphasizes that you take the goals seriously. Perhaps most important, it encourages employees to monitor their own progress and measure it when possible. When setting up a reporting system, keep in mind that it should be simple, straightforward, as well as not time-consuming.

   b. Schedule regular, short meetings with employees to discuss progress toward their goals. Believe it or not, these may be as short as five minutes—just long enough to share information about progress. These meetings should have two purposes: first, to provide a forum for basic communication so all parties know the situation, and second, to serve as opportunities to discuss barriers to performance, any things that are slowing progress toward their goals. In other words, use these meetings to identify barriers and to develop strategies to remove them. That's one of the prime roles of managers and supervisors, to work with each of their employees to build success.

c. You can also schedule group reporting meetings where information about progress is exchanged, not only between you and the employee, but among employees. This can be particularly effective in team-based work where goals are shared among members of a team. This approach works well when much of the work is arranged in "projects" and where employees are interdependent and can benefit from knowing what other staff members are doing, and how it might impact their work. Some managers devote a short segment of each staff meeting to this purpose. Keep in mind that the purpose is to improve performance and to facilitate good communication practices, not to blame people. Focus on improvement and identifying and removing barriers to performance.

3. *Use informal methods for communication about goals.*
Some managers prefer less formal means of communicating about performance goals. Often more formal, scheduled methods aren't necessary. It's quite possible to have occasional, short discussions without scheduling them. Some people refer to this process as "management by walking around," and the process is simple.

Allocate some of your work time to chatting with employees in informal ways. Visit with employees and ask questions. You'll be amazed at how much you can accomplish. Drop by their work stations. Talk at coffee breaks. That kind of thing can provide great results.

What questions can you ask? It's good to start with general ones. Here are some examples:

■ How are things going?
■ Is there anything I can do to help you on the [XYZ] project?

■ Are you noticing anything that's slowing down your work that I can help you with?

■ What do you need from me so things go more smoothly?

Notice that we've phrased these questions in a "helping way," not in a way that might be construed as threatening. That's important. You don't want to give the impression that you are snooping or conducting some sort of sneaky inquisition. Take the position that you are there to help. That will encourage employees to tell you the truth and give you the information you need to offer help.

It's also important that you avoid "micromanaging" in these conversations. That means that you should avoid "looking over the employees' shoulder" and telling them how they should be doing their work. It's OK to offer occasional suggestions, but if you micromanage in these informal conversations, staff are going to stop being open in communicating with you. Remember that these informal conversations allow you to stay informed without being intrusive, and afford an opportunity for you to help employees meet their performance goals. Don't be overbearing or staff will shut down.

Using Goals for Evaluation and Appraisal

By the time performance reviews and evaluations roll around, there should be nothing that you and the employees need to discuss in those meetings that you haven't been discussing throughout the year. That brings us to the following suggestions to help you use performance goals in the evaluation process.

Prepare for Appraisal Meetings

Appraisal meetings work best when both parties are prepared and know what to expect. Proper preparation means that appraisal meetings can be shorter and less stressful. There are several ways of preparing.

First, ensure that employees understand the purpose of the appraisal meetings. Most employees have had some unpleasant experiences with performance reviews and may bring some unpleasant baggage that interferes with good communication. The first step is to talk to employees prior to the meeting and explain why you are doing it and what to expect. Here are some basic points to cover:

- The meeting is to review performance for the purpose of helping the employee succeed in the future.
- There will be no surprises, since there will be nothing discussed in the review meeting that hasn't already been discussed during the year.
- Both employee and manager have input into the process: the opinions and perceptions of both are important.

Describe the process you will be using for the meeting—an agenda, if you like. Here are some possible items:

- Review the employee's major job responsibilities and discuss how they relate to the goals of the organization.
- Go through each of the employee's major goals to determine whether he or she has achieved them.
- Identify any problems or barriers the employee has experienced in achieving the goals.
- Identify strategies and plans to remove performance barriers.
- Complete any forms and documentation as needed.
- Begin the process of setting goals for the next year.

Once you and the employee understand the purposes and conduct of the performance appraisal meeting, it's time to determine how you and the employee should prepare for it. To reduce the time needed for the meeting, you might ask the employee to review his or her goals for the past year and make notes on how he or she feels the work has gone. You can do the same thing. You might also both review the employee's job description to see if it is still accurate and review the appraisal form you will be using in the meeting. Add preparation elements as you see fit.

Take on a Facilitative Role in Evaluations

During performance appraisals, you want to create a state of affairs that encourages each employee to evaluate his or her performance. One reason we use performance goals is to make it easier for employees to do so, during the year and at appraisal time. You need to take on the role of questioner and enabler rather than judge and jury. That's not to say you can't offer opinions, suggestions, and an occasional judgment and it doesn't mean you have to agree with the employee's self-evaluation. After all, you still have your managerial responsibilities and obligations. It does mean that your starting point in evaluations is to ask the employee to assess how well he or she has done in achieving his or her goals.

Base Discussions on the Performance Goals

Since you've gone to the trouble of creating performance goals, use them. Most of the discussions during performance appraisal should relate directly to whether the employee has achieved his or her goals and what factors have impeded or helped. That means that you shouldn't introduce extraneous observations about performance during the performance appraisal meeting. It's not fair, for example, to criticize an employee for doing or not doing something, when there is no reference to that thing in his or her performance goals.

Focus on the Discussion, Not the Form

While you may be responsible for completing an evaluation form, don't let that drive the appraisal process. Remember that the ultimate purpose of the whole thing is to improve performance. Forms don't perform. Neither do they improve performance. People do. Focus on identifying whether employees have met their goals. If not, discuss the reasons and ways to ensure they will meet them in the future.

Eliminate Blame

Performance appraisal meetings can focus on the past and on blame or they can focus on the present and future, on solving problems and creating success. It's up to you. Keep in mind that, while employees need to be held accountable for performance, you can't change the past and you won't improve performance by spending your time blaming the employee. The appraisal process is a problem-solving process. Use the past to inform your decisions about engineering success in the future. Focus on diagnosis and fixing things, not blaming, embarrassing, or humiliating employees.

Conclusion

By now you should have a good understanding of what performance goals are for, what they look like, and how to use them to guide and improve the performance of employees and the company in general. If you "keep your eyes on the prize," the positive benefits of having and using performance goals properly, you should be able to harness the power of goal setting to make your own life easier while improving your managerial contributions to the organization.

Part Two

Perfect Phrases for Setting Performance Goals

Descriptive Contents

Work Outputs and Productivity   57

Goals in this section can be used with any employee; they pertain to maintaining and improving productivity for the individual employee, for colleagues, and for the work unit.

Personal and Skill Development   60

Goals in this section can be used with any employee; they relate to the employee improving his or her ability to contribute to the organization through acquiring skills, whether to remedy weak areas as revealed through performance appraisals or to grow in areas that would increase chances of promotion.

Communication   63

Goals in this section can be used with any employee; they relate to the processes of written and oral communication within the organization and with outside entities.

Section Two. Performance Goals for General Management Responsibilities

Managing Performance   69

Goals in this section can be used with managers and supervisors responsible for performance management and appraisal.

Communications

Goals in this section are relevant to all personnel who have staff reporting to them; these goals relate to communications within the organization and with clients.

Section Three. Performance Goals for Specific Industries and Jobs

Creative Communication

Goals in this section can be used with employees involved in creating written and graphic material in all forms—advertising copy, corporate image graphics, brochures, newsletters, and websites.

Customer Service and Support—Management

Goals in this section can be used with anyone who manages or supervises staff having customer service and support responsibilities.

Customer Service and Support

Goals in this section can be used with any employee who has direct contact with customers (both internal and external), who is involved in enhancing customer experience, or who supervises or manages employees who have direct customer contact.

Financial 97

Goals in this section can be used with anyone involved in financial management and processing financial information (e.g., accounts receivable clerks), executives and managers, and anyone directly involved in financial functions (e.g., accountants, auditors). Because financial functions are often distributed throughout different levels of the organization, goals in this section may fit those with management responsibilities and those without.

Food Preparation—Management 103

Goals in this section can be used with anyone who supervises staff involved in the preparation of food.

Food Preparation 105

Goals in this section can be used with any employees who are involved in the preparation of food that is to be directly consumed, such as cooks, chefs, bakers, and those preparing ready-to-eat meals in various contexts.

Food Services—Management 107

Goals in this section can be used for those who supervise employees involved in the food service industry, most notably those involved in catering, waiting on tables, delivering food, and maintaining eating areas.

Internet/Intranet Related   137

The Internet (general access) and the Intranet (internal access only) have become major tools for businesses whether it be as a way of communicating via e-mail with customers and between employees, or as methods to market, support customers, and monitor brands and reputation. Here you will find goals related to positions that are involved in the development, maintenance, and use of Internet and Intranet resources.

Mechanical Repair and Trades   143

Goals in this section can be used for employees directly involved in the repair of machinery of various sorts and trades like plumbing, carpentry, auto mechanics, and welding.

Physical Plant Maintenance—Management   146

Goals in this section can be used with management and supervisory staff involved in supervising maintenance, repair, and cleaning activities related to the physical space and equipment in the workplace.

Support 174

Goals in this section can be used with employees carrying out various support functions—filing, reception, switchboard, and handling phone calls.

Transit/Transportation 177

Goals in this section can be used for employees directly involved in transporting people, including public bus and school bus drivers and taxi and limousine service personnel.

Workplace Health and Safety—Management 180

Goals in this section can be used with managers, supervisors, and team leaders whose reports deal directly with workplace health and safety programs and issues.

Workplace Health and Safety 183

Goals in this section can be used with employees responsible for managing and implementing workplace health and safety programs and issues, work teams with similar responsibilities, and individuals.

Section One

Performance Goals for Any Position

Readiness for Work

Use goals in this section for any employee when there has been a current or past issue related to the topic. Most employees understand they are expected to arrive at work on time and ready for work, so it's unnecessary to set such goals with them unless there has been a problem. These are goals used to remediate an existing problem.

Punctuality

- Arrive at work on time 98% of the time.
- Arrive at meetings on time so as not to inconvenience other participants.
- Return from breaks on time 98% of the time.
- Notify your supervisor at least one hour before scheduled arrival if you anticipate arriving late.
- Clock in and out in accordance with company procedures 100% of the time.
- Begin working within five minutes of arriving at work.
- Arrive on time for meetings with customers 98% of time.
- Do not cause *any* customer to wait more than 15 minutes due to lateness.
- Do not lose *any* customer due to lateness.
- Do not cause more than one verified customer complaint due to lateness.

Attendance and Absenteeism

- Limit less serious health-related absences to seven days per year.
- Use sick days only for health reasons or for other reasons approved by supervisor in advance.
- Provide documentation, as required in company policy, for any absences greater than three consecutive work days.

- Arrange in advance with supervisor for any absences not related to health (e.g., child care).
- Notify supervisor of emergency absences as soon as possible.

Health
- Ensure that there are zero instances of arriving at work under the influence of alcohol or drugs.
- Notify manager of any on-the-job injuries as soon as possible, preferably within 24 hours.
- Wash hands each time before and after meals, breaks, and arriving at work.
- Cooperate with manager and/or employee assistance programs to rearrange job responsibilities as required by health issues.
- Attend regular alcohol counseling sessions as agreed upon as condition of employment.
- Participate in the drug-testing program as agreed upon.
- Stay home (away from work) if experiencing flu-like symptoms.
- Attend employee assistance meetings as agreed upon with manager.

See also: Self-Management and Work Habits

Conflict Management and Team Contributions

Goals in this section can be used with any employee; they focus on desirable methods of dealing with conflict and how the employee can contribute to better team functioning. Many of these are process-driven rather than results driven. While you CAN focus only on team results, this is often shortsighted. When conflict and team issues are not managed properly within the group, the group may still achieve its results, but only for a short time. Process goals can be instrumental in preventing measurable productivity losses. Also because different groups differ in terms of what they need to work effectively, team and conflict goals are sometimes difficult to specify without knowing the particular group.

Tip: When working with employee to set these goals, drill down so employee understands what they mean in terms of his or her behavior.

Contributions to Team Health

- Intervene in group discussions when discussion seems to create embarrassment or belittles other team members.
- Play facilitating role in team meetings to encourage other team members to participate.
- Give credit to others who contribute to team well-being.
- Model desirable team behavior to the satisfaction of the manager.
- Balance task and process so work gets done and positive team climate is maintained.
- Advocate the "celebration" of different talents of team members and capitalize on those talents to make the team more effective.

- Move between leadership role and team member role on various projects, as required.
- Establish solid rapport with each team member, as indicated by team members.
- Refrain from gossip or other discussions about fellow team members behind their backs.
- Redirect group conversation away from gossip.

Contributions to Team Productivity

- Generate at least two ideas per year that help the team improve productivity.
- Initiate group discussion for process improvement.
- Learn and teach the use of control charts to team members.
- Encourage others on the team to identify barriers to team functioning and to suggest remedies.
- Perform team-assigned work on time and to standards.
- Coordinate own responsibilities with those of other team members so no project is delayed due to lack of team coordination.

Handling Customer Conflicts

- Use active listening techniques when customer complaints are directed your way.
- Address problems with customers so manager need not be involved 95% of the time.
- Resolve 99% of customer conflicts within 24 hours of the initial conflicted interaction and to the customer's satisfaction.
- Handle customer conflicts in calm, unemotional, and helpful ways, to the satisfaction of the manager.
- Refer a customer to the manager in cases when the conflict is not resolvable at your level.

- Ensure that the customer recognizes that the employee is trying to resolve the problem.
- Receive zero customer complaints regarding lack of effort to resolve disagreements.

Handling Internal Conflicts

- Address peers privately when critiquing work at hand.
- Handle provocation in ways that de-escalate conflict situations.
- Deal with differences of opinion in open and respectful ways.
- Ensure that there are zero incidences of losing temper and lashing out at colleagues.
- Accept criticism from peers without becoming defensive.
- Refrain from lobbying other staff members for support in conflicts.
- Receive no valid complaints about conduct during the year from peers.
- Accept help from manager to resolve conflicts, according to manager.
- Refrain from public efforts to humiliate or embarrass colleagues who disagree.

See also: Communication, Communications, Customer Service and Support

Self-Management and Work Habits

Goals in this section can be used regardless of job. Unless there is a perceived problem, most staff do not need these included in their personal goals and objectives. The exception occurs when an employee has a tendency to ignore these assumed or implicit guidelines in the past in ways that affect performance in the workplace. For example, most employees don't require an explicit goal to encourage them to behave scrupulously and honestly, but employees with a history of behaving negligently and with little regard for the truth might benefit from setting such a goal.

Tip: Drill down to ensure employee understands the specifics expected for that employee. For example, what does "well-groomed" mean in your company and for *your* employees?

Appearance and Clothing

- Maintain well-groomed, neat appearance, to the satisfaction of your supervisor.
- Follow corporate dress code at all times.
- Arrive at work with required safety clothing and equipment in good condition.
- Ensure zero validated complaints about appearance from customers.
- Modify clothing worn to reflect the particular work tasks of the day.
- Maintain change of clothing at work when different work tasks require different attire.

Ethical/Personal Conduct

- Behave scrupulously and honestly in all activities.
- Approach manager or HR for advice when faced with

situations where the proper and ethical choice is not completely clear.

- Demonstrate integrity and honesty while interacting with customers, coworkers, and managers.
- Report any personal conflicts of interest to manager as soon as becoming aware of them and/or before others bring them to manager's attention.
- Follow all guidelines regarding ethical and proper use of company equipment, including Internet access.
- Provide visible leadership to colleagues regarding the importance of ethical conduct.
- Seek out guidance from others regarding appropriate conduct when ethical conflicts occur.
- Know and follow all applicable laws.
- Receive zero validated complaints from customers regarding dishonesty.
- Receive zero validated complaints for using company equipment for personal use without authorization.
- Limit personal use of computer and company Internet access to lunchtime or break time as per company policy.
- Missing merchandise in his department is no more than the company average.

Organization and Use of Time

- Keep personal work space tidy and well organized.
- Replace any books (or other resources) when finished to allow others to find them.
- Spend five minutes or less a day on personal phone calls.
- Schedule vacation time by negotiating with supervisor to mutual satisfaction.
- Adhere to company policy regarding eating and drinking at desk.

- Replace any shared equipment or resources as soon as possible.
- Ensure that others can find things you have organized or moved.
- Ensure that no more than one minute per call is spent finding a customer information file under his or her control.
- Balance work-space functionality and neatness.
- Manage multiple projects at the same time with no delays resulting from disorganization.
- Meet project milestones at least 90% of time.
- Maintain project time sheets as agreed upon with supervisor.
- Maintain billable hours according to company standards.

Willingness to Help/Volunteer
- Volunteer 75% of the time to "buddy up" with new team members.
- Volunteer 50% of the time to take team meeting minutes and publish them.
- Volunteer 50% of the time to organize after-hours social outings.
- When daily work quota is met, volunteer 100% of the time to help others meet their daily quota.
- Take responsibility for at least one United Way charity activity every three years.

See also: Readiness for Work, Work Outputs and Productivity, Conflict Management, and Team Contributions

Work Outputs and Productivity

Goals in this section can be used with any employee; they pertain to maintaining and improving productivity for the individual employee, for colleagues, and for the work unit.

Tip: As with many goal categories, using specific, measurable goals is preferred, but do not neglect less specific process goals (the way things are done) that are hard to measure when and if it's been demonstrated that a process needs attention.

Own Work

- Develop and implement at least one cost-saving idea applicable to your own work each year.
- Redesign the file system to reduce file retrieval time by 10%.
- Increase your processing speed by at least 10% by August 20XX.
- Improve the profit margin on items sold by 12% this year.
- Seek out advice from supervisor for ways to improve work quality and quantity.
- Upsell successfully with minimum of 3% of customers.
- Complete all major assigned projects on time and within budget.
- Accept responsibility for quantity and quality of work without blaming others for problems.
- Balance the demands of multiple projects so no project falls behind schedule.
- Ensure that outputs are free of defects by the time they reach the customer.

- Produce outputs that meet agreed-upon standards 98% of time.

Contributing to Work of Others

- Ensure that your actions do not interfere with coworkers or reduce their productivity as indicated by zero validated complaints to manager from coworkers.
- Spend minimum of two hours per month assisting other staff increase their productivity.
- Participate in sales support meeting by offering at least one sales tip per meeting to other attendees.
- Inform coworkers if you become aware of issues that may affect their productivity.
- Ensure that resources used (e.g., books, tools, manuals, supplies) are returned to their proper place so others can use them.
- Refrain from interrupting the work of others for social reasons.
- Respond to requests for information from coworkers within one day of request.
- Inform support staff when unavailable for phone calls so they can inform callers of the approximate call-back time.
- Refrain from avoiding work and passing it off to coworkers.
- Encourage coworkers and recognize their contributions.
- Provide feedback and suggestions to peers without being intrusive or overbearing.
- Coach others in developing sensible goals.
- Document and communicate about shared work so others have information they need to be productive.

Contributing to Overall Productivity

- Contribute via the suggestion system at least one useable idea for improving productivity every six months.

- Generate at least one cost-cutting idea that is implemented and does not reduce quality.
- Modify individual work to reflect changes in current work-unit priorities.
- Prioritize your own work according to work-unit priorities.
- Volunteer for tasks outside of job responsibilities to help the work unit achieve its goals.
- Lead the improvement team in reducing errors by 12% this year.
- Lead explaining basics of social media by spending a minimum of one hour per month teaching or helping coworkers to use social media for work.
- Identify and help others identify root causes, using company continuous improvement tools.

See also: Self-Management and Work Habits, Conflict Management and Team Contributions, Productivity/Process Improvement/Organizational Results

Personal and Skill Development

Development of personal and work-related skills is a shared responsibility where both employer and employee need to take initiative. Goals in this section apply to any employee. They relate to the employee improving his or her ability to contribute to the organization through acquiring skills, whether to remedy weak areas as revealed through performance appraisals or to grow in areas that would increase chances of promotion.

Assessment

- Identify the two most important specific skill gaps that might impede work performance and suggest possible actions to address.
- Determine at least one means (formal and/or informal) to close each of the skill gaps identified.
- Identify and communicate career goals to manager and develop a career development plan, to be updated each year.
- Choose one new skill to acquire that will expand your current abilities to prepare you for other responsibilities and specify the outcomes you expect.
- Target one aspect of personal development and specify criteria by which coworkers will assess your growth in that area.

Formal Learning

- Research training options to identify the most cost-effective training methods for each of the areas identified for development.
- Attend at least one work-related training seminar per year.

- Attend evening or weekend classes as agreed upon with supervisor and as identified as important for promotion.
- Earn at least a B grade in all company-sponsored college courses.
- Attend one annual professional conference in your field and prepare a report for others in the company.
- Satisfy all conditions required to maintain licensing in your field.
- Report on any formal training attended within one week of completion, and make recommendations.
- Abide by any agreements made with the company regarding return of service for training.
- Receive zero validated complaints about conduct in seminars and training attended.

Informal Learning
- Seek out coaching from more experienced staff members to build your skills.
- Share new skills with coworkers doing similar jobs.
- Request help from the manager before your productivity is negatively affected by insufficient knowledge.
- Communicate that you are willing to receive feedback from supervisors and coworkers.
- Ask others for suggestions about how to do something more efficiently.
- Take the initiative for learning by researching and reading independently and then submitting a written summary to the manager by the end of each month, listing the main research sources used, the articles and books read, and outlining what you learned from each.
- Demonstrate initiative when unable to accomplish a task, by consulting manuals before calling for help.

- Show interest in professional development by using personal time for development activities when appropriate.
- Ensure zero instances of problems resulting from not reading product instructions.

See also: Work Outputs and Productivity

Communication

Communication is the lifeblood of effective organizations, so goals in this section can be used with any employee. They include the processes of written and oral communication within the organization and with outside entities, including customers, suppliers, regulatory bodies, and also other departments or people within one's own organization.

Interpersonal/Team

- Communicate with respect with others in the organization, regardless of their status.
- Accept feedback from others without becoming defensive.
- Provide feedback to others that conforms to general feedback rules regarding tone and timing.
- Reduce the need for others to require clarification resulting from unclear communication.
- Zero work errors verified as a result of being unclear in communicating.
- Speak persuasively, using facts and figures, not emotion, to support position.
- Refrain from ad hominem attacks.
- Draft internal documents free of typographical and spelling errors.
- Refrain from telling jokes based on sex, race, religion, physical characteristics, or profanity.
- Contribute to team communication in meetings by bringing discussions back to the topic when they digress.
- Use most effective communication channel depending on content/issue.
- Use face-to-face communication when issues involve emotional content.

Management

- Provide essential information to manager as requested and on time.
- Zero occurrence of manager lacking critical information in order to answer executive queries.
- Inform management of problems before they affect productivity.
- Report any anticipated variances from schedules to management at least one month in advance.
- Listen to improvement suggestions offered by manager and act upon them.
- Respond to management requests for information within 24 hours.
- Document customer concerns and forward to management promptly.
- Draft required reports for management on time and with no need for revisions.

Customers

- Inform customers of unavoidable delays.
- Explain to the customer's satisfaction why his or her needs cannot be met.
- Project an image of patience and expertise to customers.
- Refrain from using pressure or coercion when communicating with customers.
- Follow up all oral agreements with written summaries to the customer within four days of oral agreement.
- Communicate with customers in plain language, to the satisfaction of the customers, as indicated by feedback.
- Ensure that the customer understands what you are saying so that he or she and you are on the same page at the conclusion of the meeting.

- Interpret the language of contracts into plain language so the customer understands, so there are no contractual disputes involving employee communication.
- Notify customers of any changes to schedules that affect them, to avoid unnecessary inconvenience.

Media Relations

- Direct all media inquiries to the appropriate media relations person, as designated.
- Refrain from any public comment on issues beyond the scope of your communication authority.
- Respond to media requests for information in appropriate fashion within one day.
- Project a positive corporate image even when provoked by media.
- Draft clear, understandable press releases that require no further clarification of the facts.
- Appear on local television shows to discuss the company at least once every three months.
- Respect confidentiality in all dealings with the media.
- Communicate a calm demeanor when under pressure.

See also: Communications, Customer Service and Support

Section Two

Performance Goals for General Management Responsibilities

Managing Performance

Goals in this section can be used with managers and supervisors responsible for performance management and appraisal.

Setting Performance Goals

- Meet with all reports to discuss and negotiate annual performance goals a minimum of twice a year.
- Set performance goals with employees in compliance with the company format and by the October 1 deadline.
- Prepare employees for the goal-setting process to ensure that they can be equal participants at least two weeks prior to goal-setting meeting.
- Inform all employees of major work-unit goals prior to the process of setting individual goals.
- Ensure that all reports understand their major job responsibilities, as indicated by annual survey results on items __, __, and __.
- Set goals that take into account individual strengths and weaknesses.
- Zero complaints from employees to HR about lack of clarity of job expectations.
- Modify goals throughout the year in response to changes in work-unit priorities.
- Ensure that goals are in place for each employee by January 6th of each year.
- Ensure that goals are directly linked to unit objectives for the year.

Communicating about Performance

- Develop a method for staying informed about progress toward goals and barriers to achieving goals.

- Provide monthly feedback to employees about ways to improve performance and summarize meetings to own manager.
- Inform human resources of any possible performance problems that may require their involvement at least one month before intervention is required.
- Identify and implement strategies to remedy performance difficulties.
- Identify with each employee any factors interfering with achieving performance goals.
- Develop with each employee strategies to remove blocks to achieving goals.
- Apply a progressive discipline process as required and in accordance with the organization's policy.
- Ensure that every employee receives at least one interim review during the year.
- Address performance problems early so they do not escalate into major problems.

Observing and Documenting

- Document any significant performance-related discussions.
- File a copy of performance goals so it can be found easily and is accessible by manager, employee, and HR.
- Maintain all performance-related documentation in accordance with corporate privacy policy with zero exceptions or breaches of privacy.
- Send a copy of the final performance appraisal to human resources by the deadline.
- Ensure that documentation is sufficiently detailed to explain disciplinary action to a third party.
- Share all documentation with the employee and make sure that the employee signs off on each document.

- For each employee, make recommendations about salary increments to human resources two weeks prior to his or her anniversary date.
- Ensure that no personnel decisions are overturned due to a lack of documentation or inadequate documentation.

Performance Appraisal/Review

- Explain the appraisal process to employees in a way that stresses common benefit.
- Make the review useful to employees, as indicated by employee comments and surveys.
- Use performance goals as a basis for the performance review.
- Identify at least two areas in which employees can improve next year.
- Augment written forms as necessary to ensure a complete performance picture.
- Give and receive feedback and information about how the employee and the work unit can improve performance.
- Ensure that there are no surprises for any employee during the review meeting.
- Use performance appraisal information as a basis for planning performance for next period.
- Identify at least one action the manager can take to help the employee do his or her job.

See also: Leadership and Organizational Climate, Productivity/Process Improvement/Organizational Results

Planning

Goals in this section can be used with managers and supervisors responsible for planning of all kinds—financial, personnel, strategic, and projects.

Financial Planning

- Develop a five-year plan every year, projecting income and costs, and present it to the VP of finance each January 15th.
- Provide a work-unit budget for each year that is within 10% of actuals.
- Plan expenditures to minimize financial risk to company.
- Identify and plan for capital expenditures that will provide a return on total investment within two years.
- Provide integrated cost and schedule control systems, thereby providing tools to meet the project's financial goals.
- Develop financial plans that superiors consider useful for making decisions.
- Communicate financial plans to staff so they can use them in making decisions.
- Forecast financial expenditures for upcoming year, separating out mandatory and discretionary spending.

Personnel Planning

- Identify at least two employees per year to be groomed for supervisory positions and create development plans for them.
- Identify alternatives to hiring new staff to cover increased workload and submit suggestions to coordinating chair of staffing committee on deadline.
- Communicate anticipated personnel needs to human resources three months prior to point at which action is required.

- Identify for layoffs staff members whose loss will affect work-unit production the least.
- Maintain a stable staff complement that is sustainable (no layoffs) in varying economic conditions.
- Promote at least one current employee each year into a supervisory position.
- Assist employees with career-development strategies and use acting status appointments and temporary assignments in other positions to develop employees for increased responsibility.
- Identify reasons for high staff turnover in the work unit and develop an action plan for reducing it.

Strategic and Work-Unit Planning

- Prepare work-unit summary and/or environmental scan for use in the company strategic planning meetings.
- With staff, develop work-unit strategic plan that reflects the larger organization's strategic goals.
- Attend the company strategic planning meetings with the material needed.
- Define clear and achievable work-unit goals that will contribute to company success.
- Develop action plans for achieving each work-unit goal that include timelines and specify individual accountabilities.
- Revise strategic work-unit plan in the event that major shifts occur in the market, the economy, and/or the environment.
- Attend annual conferences so as to be able to predict future trends in the industry.

Work Planning/Scheduling

■ Assign critical projects to the most qualified and appropriate employees as reflected in on-time completion rates.

■ Ensure that all major projects are completed according to planned estimates.

■ Plan work to minimize overtime by 5%.

■ Ensure cost overruns are limited to 2% of overall project budget.

■ Ensure that all employees have the skills needed to achieve their work goals, as indicated by the employees in annual employee survey.

■ Balance staff workloads so that more projects are completed on time this year than last.

See also: Personnel/Hiring/Retention

Personnel/Hiring/Retention

Goals in this section can be used with managers and supervisors who are involved in workforce planning, hiring candidates, and ensuring that the best employees are retained.

Employee Retention

- Ensure that employees who are not performing to standards either improve within three months of notification by their manager or are terminated.

- Ensure that key, valuable employees are identified by their managers and retained at a rate of at least 90%.

- Research salaries to ensure that offers are attractive enough to retain valuable employees but within 20% of industry average in the locale.

- Address organizational issues identified in exit meetings that may contribute to above-average turnover rates.

- Ensure that your managerial behavior does not contribute to loss of key employees as indicated in exit interviews.

- Provide sufficient work challenges for younger, high-potential employees, to rate at least 4 out of 5 for "work challenges" on surveys of employees hired within last three years.

- Develop career development plans with high-value employees to reduce turnover of "management designated" employees to no more than 5% per year.

- Ensure that 85% of new hires are retained past the probationary period.

- Maintain employee turnover rate at 10% less than industry average.

Forecasting

- Provide workforce need projections to human resources by Dec. 1 of each year.
- Ensure that personnel forecasts are accurate enough that no layoffs will be necessary unless revenue drops by more than 15% year on year.
- Identify skills needed for the upcoming year and ensure that employees have those skills so there are zero delays as a result of skills lacking.
- Identify alternate strategies (e.g., outsourcing) to meet forecast personnel needs within personnel budget.
- Ensure that no projects are delayed due to lack of staff or lack of staff skill.

Interviewing

- Follow the required interview protocol 100% of the time.
- Take relevant notes in interviews so decisions can be justified with specifics and make those notes available to HR, regulatory agencies, or executives as required.
- Contribute to creating a professional interview environment in which candidates feel comfortable, as indicated on follow-up surveys.
- Use behavioral interviewing techniques as outlined by company procedures.
- Refrain from dominating interviews when there are other interviewers.
- Provide sufficient opportunity for job candidate to demonstrate knowledge and abilities.
- Ensure that zero validated complaints are received regarding illegal interview questions.
- Arrive at interviews on time and ready to be an active and effective interviewer.

- Prepare for all interviews as evidenced by asking relevant and useful questions.
- During interviews, refrain from acting on any personal biases that are not job-related.
- Refrain from canceling or rescheduling interviews except for valid health reasons.
- Ensure that contributions and questions are consistent across interviews for any one position.
- Assess all candidates using the required point system.

Preparing for Hiring

- Update job descriptions at least once a year so they reflect the actual work done.
- Work with human resources to develop ads that attract highly qualified candidates.
- Ensure that all specified job qualifications are legal and do not contravene EEOC regulations.
- Develop a general plan for bringing new hires up to speed quickly.
- Cooperate with human resources to develop strategies to expand the pool of minority applicants.
- Ensure that all involved human resources staff are clear about work-unit needs for every position to be filled.
- Assist human resources staff in classifying each position accurately to reflect skill and responsibility requirements.
- Collaborate with human resources staff to establish for each position a fair salary level that will attract desirable candidates.
- Help human resources staff set point values for all qualifications for every position to be filled.

See also: Planning, Human Resources and Personnel—Management

Leadership and Organizational Climate

Goals in this section can be used with managers, supervisors, and team leaders who are expected to demonstrate leadership within their organizations and contribute to the development and maintenance of a healthy and productive work climate.

Communication

- Align verbal and nonverbal language in a consistent manner.
- Balance listening and speaking to demonstrate an interest in others' thoughts and feelings.
- Proactively seek out both bad and good news from peers and employees regularly and systematically.
- Speak with and listen to at least eight employees each month, to create person-to-person relationships.

Personal and Staff Development

- Create a "teachable vision"—a vision of the future that everyone in the company can grasp and understand as indicated by each employee's ability to articulate the vision when asked.
- Seek coaching and mentoring from other effective leaders, both within and outside the organization.
- Conduct a leadership self-assessment every year.
- Identify at least one leadership skill gap and develop and implement a plan to remedy the gap.
- Coach and mentor at least one staff member who has leadership potential.

Work Climate

- Make realistic promises and keep them.
- Develop a flexible budgeting system to permit employees to make some financial decisions on their own.

- Provide clear goals to staff and leave it up to them to determine how to attain the goals.
- Sponsor yearly surveys of employees to determine their perceptions of organizational climate.
- Develop and implement an action plan to improve employee perceptions of trust.
- Identify and correct situations where work-unit actions are inconsistent with unit vision or corporate values.
- Hold yourself and the employees accountable for actions and results without looking for someone to blame when things go wrong.
- Focus on the present and the future and encourage staff to do so.
- Make decisions based on "the big picture" and the demands of the current problems.
- Identify the best and brightest employees and retain at least 90% of those so designated.
- Take personal risks by being authentic, open, and honest as determined by executive mentor.
- Improve employee job satisfaction ratings by 20% next year.
- Recognize employee contributions publicly and privately and share the spotlight for successes.
- Focus on action and timing and avoid "analysis paralysis."
- Show confidence in staff by delegating important work to them.

See also: Communication, Productivity/Process Improvement/ Organizational Results

Productivity/Process Improvement/ Organizational Results

Goals in this section can be used for managers and supervisors and are related to responsibilities for improving productivity, becoming more cost-effective, and contributing to the overall results of the company.

Productivity

- Increase total work-unit output by 3% this year.
- Reduce labor costs by 3% in work unit without lowering output.
- Increase profit margin by 3% per year without negatively impacting customer satisfaction.
- Research and identify possible capital investments required to update equipment to improve productivity.
- Ensure that any capital expenditures to increase productivity achieve complete cost recovery within three years.
- Identify and provide for staff training as needed to improve productivity.
- Engage staff in identifying and implementing strategies to improve productivity.
- Set yearly productivity improvement goals and communicate them to all staff.
- Ensure that each employee understands his or her role with respect to improving productivity for work unit.
- Ensure that no productivity is lost as a result of employees being unclear about work-unit priorities.
- Delegate authority to employees so they can respond to productivity barriers quickly or immediately without requiring further approvals.
- Reduce by three weeks the time it takes new hires to become fully productive.

- Identify any staff members whose productivity is below average and use performance management procedures to help staff members improve.
- Monitor staff and take action if any employees appear to be lowering the productivity of their colleagues.

Process Improvement

- Educate all staff in the use of process improvement and basic statistical tools.
- Create a climate so employees at all levels feel comfortable enough to offer process improvement suggestions to managers.
- Monitor statistical reports on process problems in order to improve process.
- Implement local suggestion box system that generates at least one process improvement idea per month that is implemented.
- Communicate proactively with employees to help remove barriers to improvement.
- Identify root causes for problems, as demonstrated by productivity improvements resulting from correct diagnosis and remediation strategy.
- Contribute in an active way to the company's process improvement team.
- Request assistance from executive managers when a process improvement requires their approvals.
- Model for employees the importance of a continuous improvement philosophy.
- Use performance management to improve processes rather than assign blame for errors.

Organizational Results

- Ensure that the work unit achieves goals and objectives for critical responsibilities.

- Proactively provide executive managers with the information they need to prioritize expenditures to improve company results.
- Subordinate the work unit's budgets and needs to the improvement needs of the organization.
- Provide input into any overall downsizing strategy to minimize the negative impacts on company productivity.
- Coordinate with other managers to reduce duplication of effort or wasted effort.
- Identify and recommend actions that will result in cost savings for the company through outsourcing.
- Become a company resource for teaching other managers about applying process improvement tools.

See also: Work Outputs and Productivity

Communications

Goals in this section are relevant to all personnel who have staff reporting to them; these goals relate to communications within the organization and with clients.

Downward

- Communicate work-unit goals to staff so they understand the bigger picture.
- All employees can explain their roles in the organization and how they can contribute if asked.
- Zero complaints from staff about having work impacted by lack of management communication.
- Operate on "want to know" rather than "need to know" in terms of what is communicated to employees.
- Explain why, not just how, things are done a certain way, so employees can explain why they do things to other employees if asked.
- Create communication climate so employees are comfortable questioning and challenging decisions.
- Provide feedback that majority of employees feel is fair and constructive as indicated by annual HR survey on feedback.

Customers/Clients

- Make final approvals on any written/promotional material seen by customers so no customers complain about errors or misleading information in promotional material.
- Resolve 80% of phone calls from angry clients on first call and to the satisfaction of the client.
- Collect customer satisfaction data by contacting at least five customers per month.
- Communicate bad news to clients effectively and respectfully.

Peers

- Refrain from withholding information from other managers that is important for their success as indicated by zero comments about this in weekly management troubleshooting meetings.

- Coordinate work with other units to reduce duplication of effort.

- Apply a consultative process when project involves decisions that may affect other work units.

- Participate actively in division management meetings and chair the meetings at least once every six months.

- Maintain effective communication with all division managerial peers regardless of personal feelings.

- Use effective communication techniques to address conflicts with peers.

- Eliminate any need for involvement by the vice president to resolve conflicts with managerial peers.

Upward

- Communicate so there are no surprises to managers higher in the hierarchy.

- Inform your manager of any events of critical importance to the satisfaction of your manager.

- Prepare and submit all reports as required, on time.

- Identify and communicate sales shortfalls at least one month before end of quarter.

- Suggest at least two cost-saving initiatives each quarter to your manager.

See also: Communication, Customer Service and Support

Section Three

Performance Goals for Specific Industries and Jobs

Creative Communication

Goals in this section can be used with employees involved in creating written and graphic material in all forms—advertising copy, corporate image graphics, brochures, newsletters, and websites.

Copywriting

- Produce copy satisfactory to the client within one revision cycle.
- Write ad copy that highlights key product selling points as specified by marketing.
- Produce three publishable articles per month.
- Create copy with no more than one factual error needing correction.
- Meet copy deadlines as specified by the director.
- Produce copy that meets space guidelines as specified by word count.
- Ensure that all material used complies with copyright laws; obtain permission when necessary.
- Modify writing style to suit client needs as indicated by client satisfaction ratings.

Copyediting/Layout

- Ensure that final copy is completely free of errors.
- Provide feedback to writers on style and quality of copy.
- Meet all deadlines for submitting final copy to production.
- Ensure that all copy contains strong lead and graphic elements.
- Work with graphics department to ensure that copy and graphics reinforce message.
- Ensure that final copy reflects desired corporate image.
- Lay out documents so they are attractive and easy to read.

Graphic Design

- Design graphic images that are memorable and reinforce the company brand.
- Create final graphic images in camera-ready form for production.
- Present graphic designs to client or executive for discussion at least one month prior to final deadline.
- Produce graphics that reinforce the message of the text they are to accompany.
- Help the client define the messages to be conveyed by the graphics to the satisfaction of the client.
- Create a final product that reflects creative standards and the needs and preferences of client/owner.
- Design conference displays that sales people perceive as useful in increasing sales.
- Maintain an inventory of graphic materials, supplies, and equipment as required for assigned projects.
- Translate thoughts, ideas, and images into pictures and designs to the satisfaction of the client.

Website Design

- Document website code so others can understand and work on code.
- Create a website that portrays the company in a manner that is consistent with corporate image policy.
- Ensure that the website can be updated quickly and efficiently.
- Make the website visually more appealing, according to feedback surveys of website visitors.
- Keep the content of the website fresh and up-to-date.
- Consult with department heads so their sections of the website contain accurate information.

- Ensure that costs for website hosting remain under $6,000 per year.
- Prepare the annual budget for website production and maintenance accurately within 10%.
- Obtain all necessary copyrights and permissions so that all website content is legal.
- Meet website sales quotas each year.
- Create an intranet site that is easy to navigate, so 80% of employees accessing it indicate they can find what they need quickly.
- Coordinate website contributors so website is completed on time.

See also: Communication, Communications

Customer Service and Support—Management

Goals in this section can be used with anyone who manages or supervises staff having customer service and support responsibilities. Since many managers also interact directly with customers, it's good to include relevant goals and objectives from the more general category that follows this one.

Customer Communication/Satisfaction

- Conduct monthly customer focus groups that yield at least one customer service improvement tactic each.
- Develop and implement customer feedback system by year-end.
- Ensure that customer inquiries and complaints receive an initial response within one working day.
- Ensure that 99% of customer complaints are resolved within five working days, measured from initial time of complaint.
- Improve overall customer satisfaction levels to a level of 3.9 on a 5-point scale by end of year as measured by response cards.
- Work with marketing to ensure all customers are aware of Internet-/Facebook-based options for communicating with company.
- Monitor via weekly reports mentions of company brands on Twitter and suggest strategies to improve brand perceptions.

Customer Service Improvements

- Reduce department complaint level to 3% of transactions.
- Develop strategy to use employee suggestion boxes to improve customer service.

- Elicit and implement two suggestions made by internal customers and verify with internal customers that they have improved service levels.

Customer Service Management
- Ensure that all employees can explain various merits of products to customers.
- Train all staff in operation of cash register so each employee can cover in emergencies.
- Orient new floor staff within two days of hiring.
- Schedule shifts so there are no fewer than three floor workers available at any time.
- Contact 10 customers a week to follow up on customer satisfaction levels.
- Monitor 5% of incoming calls to call center to evaluate response quality.
- Provide feedback to each employee on his or her customer-handling process at least once a month.
- Lead team to create Internet-based support community to be functional by end of first quarter.
- Implement Internet self-service strategy to result in reducing customer service staff by one position due to lessened customer service phone call load within 12 months.
- Ensure that service-call scheduling results in no more than an average delay of 10 minutes in arriving.
- Ensure that all staff members understand and apply proper phone etiquette.
- Reduce time that customers spend on hold by 10%.
- Reduce merchandise returns from present level of 3% to 2% storewide.
- Ensure that all staff can correctly apply returns and refunds policy 100% of the time.

- Accurately plan customer service loads to reduce overtime to less than 2% of total hours worked.
- Implement a system of employee recognition (for superior customer service) that majority of employees endorse.

Customer Service Quality

- Maintain at least 95% of items as "in stock" for any given month.
- Reduce checkout wait time to an average of five minutes.
- Reduce shopping cart abandonment by 5% for online shoppers by end of fiscal year.

See also: Communication, Retail/Merchandising—Management, Sales and Business Development—Management

Customer Service and Support

Goals in this section can be used with any employee who has direct contact with customers (both internal and external), who is involved in enhancing customer experience, or who supervises or manages employees who have direct customer contact. You will find there is some overlap of items between this and the previous section because in the workplace there is often some overlap of responsibilities between customer service managers and customer service providers.

Customer Communication

- Conduct/lead monthly customer focus groups that yield at least one customer service improvement tactic each.
- Provide bi-monthly report of customer service improvement tactics to manager that includes recommendations of two methods to implement to improve customer service.
- Provide a first response to direct customer-initiated contact on Twitter/Facebook within three hours of regular working hours.
- Intervene on online community support forum to answer customer support question if question remains unanswered for 24 hours.
- Moderate and post user/visitor comments made on online community support forums so all spam and abusive posts are removed (and poster warned or removed) within three hours of posting on work days.
- Develop and implement customer feedback system by year-end.
- Notify customers of changes in service-call timing at least one hour before scheduled appointment, 100% of time.

- Design and write clear and understandable product manuals, as measured by customer feedback.
- Inform other employees in contact with customer of previous conversations with that customer and the history of the situation.
- Ensure that no customer needs to repeat his or her information during ordering/support call.
- Contact each customer at least 30 days before expiration of contract to negotiate renewal.
- Contact product purchasers within 30 days of purchase to discuss service agreement options.

Customer Satisfaction/Retention

- Maintain rating average across items of at least three in customer surveys.
- Maintain at least 90% of customers returning to store.
- Receive no more than two customer complaints validated by manager per year.
- Receive no more than three customer requests per year to assign different staff member.
- Receive no more than three order cancellations per year resulting from customer service complaints.
- Ensure that 90% of customers choose to renew their contracts.
- Identify reasons why customers are not renewing and report this information to customer service manager each month.

Customer Service Improvements

- Contribute at least two customer service improvement strategies per year.
- Evaluate and report on competitors' customer service procedures.

- Reduce department complaint level to 3% of transactions.
- Develop strategy to use employee suggestion boxes to improve customer service.

Customer Service Management

- Work with new hires to train them in product knowledge so they can explain various merits of products to customers.
- Train coworkers to operate cash register so they can cover in emergencies.
- Schedule shifts so there are no fewer than three floor workers available at any time.
- Contact 10 customers a week to follow up on customer service perceptions.
- Monitor 10% of incoming calls to call center.
- Provide feedback to each employee on his or her customer-handling process at least once a month.
- Ensure that service-call scheduling results in no more than an average delay of 10 minutes in arriving.
- Ensure that all staff members understand and apply proper phone etiquette.
- Reduce time that customers spend on hold by 10%.
- Reduce merchandise returns from present level storewide.
- Accurately plan customer service loads to reduce overtime to less than 2% of total hours worked.
- Implement a system of employee recognition (for superior customer service) that majority of employees endorse.

Customer Service Quality

- Maintain at least 95% of items as "in stock" for any given month.
- Reduce checkout wait time to an average of five minutes.

- Price items so every item on shelf has price sticker/UPC.
- Fulfill all orders the same day as received.
- Process refunds without intervention/help of supervisor.
- Route phone calls to proper person 98% of the time.
- Solve customer problems in single phone call 90% of the time.
- Identify and report to superior any slowdowns in providing customer service.
- Provide at least two possible options for purchase to each customer.
- Fulfill promises to customers 100% of time or notify them of changes.
- Provide job quotes that are no more than 10% off final price.
- Answer all calls professionally, using proper phone etiquette.
- Handle customer complaints without supervisor intervention 90% of time.
- Maintain abandoned call levels to 4% of total calls.
- Do not interfere with overall customer service team performance as measured by comments from other team members.
- Provide advice to customers that works the first time in 95% of contacts.

See also: Communication, Retail/Merchandising, Sales and Business Development

Financial

Goals in this section can be used with anyone involved in financial management and processing financial information (e.g., accounts receivable clerks), executives and managers, and anyone directly involved in financial functions (e.g., accountants, auditors). Because financial functions are often distributed throughout different levels of the organization, goals in this section may fit those with management responsibilities and those without.

Bottom-Line Results

- Increase shareholder dividends by 1%.
- Increase stock market value by $10 million.
- Increase market share by 10% over next three years.
- Increase ratio of profit to sales by 10%.
- Reduce uncollectible debt by 20%.
- Maintain current AAA credit rating.
- Identify five cost-saving initiatives by midyear and implement at least two by year-end.
- Maintain return on equity at a minimum of 10% a year.

Budgeting

- Complete or oversee preparation of final yearly budget on time and with no revisions required.
- Ensure that submitted budget conforms to required format and conditions.
- Analyze and approve yearly budgets of subordinate work units four weeks prior to year-end.
- Reduce operating budget by 10% for next fiscal year.
- Present budget and obtain approval from the board of directors.
- Develop tax-reduction strategy resulting in 8% tax savings.

- Analyze costs and benefits of outsourcing and report them to the CFO, to her satisfaction.
- Budget funds in accordance with program priorities provided by the board of directors.
- Create unit budget that includes 10% cut in operating funds.
- Submit budget that requires no more than one modification cycle.
- Provide summary of budget options that includes effects of those options on overall revenue.
- Prepare budgetary predictions for next five years for use in strategic budgeting.
- Identify how corporate allocation for employee development is to be spent.
- Identify and prioritize expenditures as required, recommended, and discretionary.

Conformance to Financial Practices

- Ensure that accounting practices conform to industry standards.
- Ensure that financial reports pass auditors' inspection without major challenges.
- Ensure that financial decisions meet legal and ethical requirements.
- Provide documents to auditors within one week of request.

Spending and Financial Control

- Implement cost-saving programs to yield 10% cost reduction without reducing output.
- Reduce ratio of cost-to-collect to collected amount to 12:100.
- Reduce non-personnel operating costs by 6% while maintaining revenue.

- Develop and implement innovative cost-cutting programs for work unit.
- Contribute to cost-control team by developing company-wide cost-control strategies.
- Limit ratio of operating costs to sales to 10%.
- Partnering with auditors, identify possible unnecessary expenditures.
- Partnering with corporate managers, identify areas of redundant or overlapping responsibilities and unnecessary spending.
- With other division managers, identify possible cost savings by using outsourcing and prepare recommendation.
- With other division managers, identify functions that may be grouped together (centralized) to yield cost savings.
- Implement and evaluate cost-control strategies mandated by company and present monthly reports to project head.
- Develop and implement a plan to identify cost overruns before they occur.
- Reduce total project cost overruns to a maximum of 4% of budgeted value.
- Manage employee suggestion system to increase total saving from suggestions to 5% of operational budget or $75,000.
- Reduce overtime payments to no more than 4% of total labor/salary costs.
- Reduce total overtime hours by 25%.
- Stabilize profit levels to limit layoffs to 2% of total workforce per year.

Processing
- Accurately process and generate a minimum of 100 invoices per week with no more than a 1% error rate.

- Run payroll reports weekly, to be completed by 10 P.M. each Friday.
- Cut accounts payable checks within time limit established by vendors.
- Cut checks in a timely fashion so no interest is accrued on accounts.
- Respond to questions from payroll and accounts payable within two working days.
- Process and validate expense claims within 30 days of submission.
- Identify any problems that slow down processing, inform superior, and offer possible solutions.
- Ensure that all reports to government are delivered on time such that no penalties are incurred.
- Conduct credit checks to reduce defaults to no more than .5% of total billed.
- Write contracts to limit contract disputes to 1% of total contracts written.
- Ensure that 90% of accounts are reconciled by the end of the following month.
- Administer petty cash according to corporate spending guidelines.
- Provide accurate payroll data to IT five days prior to each check run.

Reporting and Communicating

- Prepare and submit monthly financial summaries to the satisfaction of the CFO.
- Inform superiors of anticipated revenue shortfalls and surpluses at least one month before final reporting.
- Submit financial reports that are accurate and do not require correction.

- Prepare and deliver oral presentations to the board of directors outlining fiscal health, to the satisfaction of the board.
- Provide financial projections for five-year period to be used in annual strategic planning sessions.
- Provide financial profit/loss projections that differ no more than 15% from actuals.
- Respond to employee payroll inquiries so no more than 5% need to be addressed by supervisor.
- Report anticipated cost overruns to executive for approval.
- Provide monthly profit/loss statements that do not require revision later.
- Provide monthly profit/loss projections for future quarters accurate within 10%.
- Improve financial reporting procedures by working with internal auditor.
- Deliver year-end reports on time and in proper format.

Revenue Enhancement
- Identify two new revenue streams to come online within two years.
- Increase net revenue by 10%.
- Increase gross revenue by 10%.
- Double percent of total revenue contributed by [product or service].

Other
- Reduce foreign exchange risk exposure to 5% of total equity.
- Provide financial advice to the satisfaction of the CFO.
- Negotiate with external suppliers to reduce costs and error rates.

- Implement supplier education program to help suppliers reduce their own costs.
- Implement new streamlined bid system to allow easier, more competitive bidding.
- Develop and implement plan to make the company's bids on projects more competitive.

See also: Customer Service and Support—Management, Sales and Business Development

Food Preparation—Management

Goals in this section can be used with anyone who supervises staff involved in the preparation of food.

Cleanliness/Hygiene/Safety

- Maintain for the upcoming year a record of zero instances of salmonella illnesses linked to restaurant.
- Be first to identify any health code violations and rectify before inspectors arrive.
- Respond to and resolve any inspector concerns that fall within your control within three days of receipt or as required by inspector.
- Prepare job aids and reminders for kitchen staff regarding hygiene practices and post them in visible areas.
- Ensure that all members of kitchen staff follow all hygiene practices 100% of the time.
- Ensure zero validated customer complaints about foreign objects in food.
- Maintain zero incidence of kitchen fires.

Cost-Effectiveness/Organization

- Maintain cost of ingredients for each meal to 30% of total retail cost.
- Schedule food preparation staff to reduce overtime by 20%.
- Schedule staff to meet customer demand, so no customer waits more than 15 minutes for a meal.
- Cut total costs for food preparation by 10% in 20XX.
- Reduce produce wastage/spoilage by 10%.
- Plan and order ingredients to take advantage of 10% bulk discount from suppliers.

- Ensure a sufficient supply of ingredients, so that no more than 5% of orders need to be refused due to lack of ingredients.
- Schedule produce purchases and deliveries so no produce served is older than two days.

Quality
- Prepare food so that customers rate taste and appearance on feedback forms as "above average" compared with competitors.
- Provide portions that customers perceive as appropriate in size, as indicated by customer feedback forms.
- Ensure that the portions vary no more than 5% by weight from corporate standards.
- Ensure that all completed orders are picked up within one minute.
- Ensure that all food items leave the kitchen at appropriate temperatures.
- Maintain consistency across batches: e.g., all doughnuts to be between 2.5 and 2.6 inches in diameter.
- Ensure that all meals contain proper nutritional value as outlined in the organization's food standards.

See also: Food Services—Management

Food Preparation

Goals in this section can be used with any employees who are involved in the preparation of food that is to be directly consumed, such as cooks, chefs, bakers, and those preparing ready-to-eat meals in various contexts.

Cleanliness/Hygiene/Safety

- Prepare preserves and canned goods on premises in accordance with procedures and standards from inspection board.
- Follow all safety and health guidelines 100% of the time.
- Notify manager immediately when safety and health guidelines are violated.
- Leave cooking area in spotless and hygienic condition at end of shift.
- Rectify safety issues immediately upon observation when possible.

Innovation

- Introduce two new vegetarian dishes to menu each month.
- Introduce two new featured dishes each month.
- Revise current recipes to eliminate MSG without sacrificing customer satisfaction.
- Conduct pre-meal evaluations of new product items with at least three staff members and one manager.
- Provide at least three new product item ideas to manager each quarter.

Inventory Control/Equipment

- Maintain recipe files so they can be used by other kitchen staff and replacements.
- Maintain ovens according to factory specifications.

- Inspect cooking equipment and verify that it is working and safe at start of each shift.
- Anticipate ingredient shortages and notify manager at least 24 hours before an ingredient is exhausted.
- Ensure that no more than 5% of orders need to be refused due to lack of ingredients.
- Ensure that kitchen utensils are replaced in holders at all times immediately after use.
- Sharpen cutting knives weekly.

Quality

- Cook food to customers' specifications to their satisfaction at least 90% of the time.
- Prepare food so that customers rate taste and appearance on feedback forms as "above average" compared with competitors.
- Provide portions that customers perceive as appropriate in size, as indicated by customer feedback forms.
- Ensure that the portions vary no more than 5% by weight from corporate standards.
- Ensure that all completed orders are picked up within one minute.
- Ensure that all food items leave the kitchen at appropriate temperatures.
- Maintain consistency across batches: e.g., all doughnuts to be between 2.5 and 2.6 inches in diameter.
- Ensure that all meals contain proper nutritional value as outlined in the organization's food standards.
- Arrange food on serving trays/plates so presentation is attractive and orderly.

See also: Food Services

Food Services—Management

Goals in this section can be used for those who supervise employees involved in the food service industry, most notably those involved in catering, waiting on tables, delivering food, and maintaining eating areas.

Catering

- Follow up on catering leads within one day of receiving them.

- Present food and catering options to customer in a clear, understandable way.

- Increase total catering revenue by 10% in 20XX.

- Coordinate food preparation and serving so that all meals are served on time.

- Convert at least 50% of customer inquiries and leads into confirmed contracts.

- Ensure that all visible members of the catering staff at any event are attired properly before taking the floor.

- Ensure no more than 1% of total catering billings are late or uncollectible.

- Verify that food supplies and ingredients are available and sufficient to prepare contracted meals plus 5%.

Customer Service

- Set customer service standards and communicate them to the staff.

- Ensure that there are no more than two instances per month when a customer leaves as a result of serving delays.

- Address customer complaints to the satisfaction of the customers.

- Speak with at least five customers per week to gather information about the service.

- When service is poor, offer restitution to customers to retain their business.
- Ensure that portions are acceptable to the customers without resulting in wastage.

Employee Supervision and Training

- Ensure that all staff members are properly attired for their shifts.
- Supervise staff to ensure that they follow all health procedures.
- Train all new serving staff in "our way" of serving.
- Provide feedback on service quality to each server at least once a month.
- Train all staff in the use of cash so there are no more than three errors per week that require manager involvement.
- Coach serving staff members so they do not sound wooden or over-rehearsed.

Facilities Management

- Schedule serving staff so there are always enough employees to meet customer demand.
- Ensure that no customer waits more than five minutes in the restaurant before being attended.
- Develop strategies to increase business from families to 20% of total sales.
- Order sufficient copies of menus so there is never a shortage.
- Forward marketing suggestions to the head office at least once a month.
- Supervise the menu design so it reflects the desired image.
- Monitor cooking equipment to ensure that no meals are delayed as a result of preventable equipment failures.

- Develop a staffing plan that takes into account possible staff absences and illness.
- Ensure that staff absences do not have a significant effect on the ability to serve customers promptly.
- Keep payroll records in accordance with company procedures or government filing requirements.
- Deposit daily receipts so there is no more than $200 cash on the premises at any one time.
- Secure premises at closing.

See also: Food Preparation—Management

Food Services

Goals in this section can be used for employees directly involved in the food service industry, most notably those who cater, wait on tables, deliver food, and maintain eating areas.

Environment

- Keep all table condiments fully stocked.
- Clear away dishes within three minutes of patrons leaving.
- Wear required attire and keep it clean and presentable.
- End the shift leaving the eating areas as clean as at beginning of shift.
- Respond to customer requests for spill cleanup within three minutes of request.
- Identify and report to maintenance any damage to furniture within one day of noticing it.
- Provide high chairs and other child-related items required by young diners.
- Carry order pad and pen and other necessary tools so no service is delayed for lack of tools.
- Set up tables with clean linen, napkins, and silverware so table can be returned to service within five minutes.

Order Taking/Processing

- Inform each customer of daily specials before taking the order.
- Make no more than one order-taking error per week that results in a delay in serving the correct order.
- Ensure that all cutlery and place settings are clean and proper before taking order.
- Tally bills and make no more than three errors per month that require correction at the cash register.

- Process each payment within four minutes of receiving it at the table.
- Return to take dessert and coffee orders within four minutes after the patrons finish the main course.
- Take orders on behalf of other staff members if they are delayed.
- Inform patrons of the approximate time it will take to serve orders when delays are anticipated.
- Offer patrons water as part of the process of greeting them and taking their order.
- Greet each patron with spiel and a friendly smile.
- Make wine suggestions that are appropriate for the meals ordered.

Serving

- Serve food according to the procedures set by the supervisor.
- Return to each table within five minutes of initial serving to inquire about customer needs.
- Ensure that no customer waits more than five minutes after finishing eating to receive bill.
- Serve every food item within two minutes of being notified that it's "up."
- Identify any errors in food orders before serving items to customer.
- Serve food in an unobtrusive manner consistent with customer expectations.
- Offer coffee refills when cups become two-thirds empty.
- Remove plates within five minutes after the patrons finish their meal.
- Handle complaints about food quality service by immediately bringing them to the attention of the manager.

See also: Food Preparation

Human Resources and Personnel—Management

Goals in this section can be used with anyone working in human resource departments who has supervisory or managerial responsibilities.

Compensation/Benefits

- Ensure that salary and benefits packages are competitive to attract top-quality candidates, according to unit managers.
- Ensure that compensation levels are within 10% of industry norms.
- Keep project salary costs for next year within 5% of estimates.
- Research and suggest options for new profit-sharing program.
- Ensure that no more than 5% of job offers are rejected due to inadequate salary and benefits.
- Maintain overall overtime levels at less than 4% of total payroll per month.
- Contribute to corporate team investigating health insurance options and write the final report for executive management.
- Identify best practices in providing day care and recommend to the board of directors a course of action that takes into account practicality and financial issues.

Conformance

- Ensure that hiring practices conform to Equal Employment Opportunity Commission requirements.
- Reduce substantiated discrimination complaints to zero.
- Inform the CEO of potential illegal practices that put the company at risk.

- Procure expert legal advice on behalf of the company as needed.
- Complete human resources audit once every two years to determine conformance levels.
- Identify any illegal nonconformance to HR laws before external agencies do.

Hiring

- Ensure that job applications are representative of the diversity of the local workforce.
- Develop strategies to increase qualified applications from members of minority groups by 10% next year.
- Keep recruitment costs within 10% of industry average.
- Fill all jobs within six weeks of initial job posting.
- Reduce the time needed to fill vacancies by 10% from previous year.

Labor Relations

- Reduce union labor actions to zero, while staying within financial guidelines.
- Reduce total grievances to 15 or fewer a year.
- Reduce total grievance proceedings losses to three per year.
- Reduce by 20% the time needed to come to labor agreements.
- Report bargaining deadlocks to the CFO within three hours of occurrence.

Policy Development/Communication

- Prepare estimates of required staffing levels for next five years, to the satisfaction of the CFO.
- Research and report on potential outsourcing of HR functions, to the satisfaction of the CFO.

- Respond to requests from senior executives for advice or information within one working day.
- Develop a downsizing strategy that does not result in significant loss in productivity.

Privacy and Confidentiality

- Lead in developing corporate policy on protecting customer and employee privacy that is in accordance with all legal requirements and ethical best practice standards in the industry to result in policy ratified by executive committee by January 5, 20XX.
- Train and designate a minimum of two human resources staff in the application of the privacy and confidentiality policy.
- Maintain a zero rate of confidential information leaks.
- Consult with other departmental managers to advise them on implementing practices to protect private and confidential data.
- Develop proactive privacy and confidentiality audit team to visit each department to audit practices, at least once every two years.

Staff Development

- With senior executives, prepare an annual staff development plan linked to the organization's strategic plan.
- Ensure that staff development planning is linked to work-unit performance management process.
- Develop a staff development plan that reflects the organization's skill needs for the upcoming year and incorporates input from executives, line managers, and employees.
- Keep current and knowledgeable about current HR trends and laws by attending annual government briefings on HR law and attending one national HR conference per year.

- Reduce staff development costs while increasing staff development hours delivered, by coordinating needs and solutions across the company and using economy of scale.
- Reduce percentage of training given in classrooms by 30% while increasing use of alternative e-learning methods.
- Manage e-learning courseware development to ensure new courseware is delivered on time and per contract specifications.

Staff Retention/Promotion

- Ensure that at least 95% of promoted employees succeed, as reflected in yearly performance reviews.
- Keep staff turnover ratio between 5% and 8% per year.
- Reduce new hire turnover to less than 10%.
- Reduce dismissals related to substance abuse to less than 3% of total dismissals.
- Reduce staff loss resulting from "insufficient challenge in job" by 10%.

Staff Satisfaction

- Chair employee satisfaction committee that suggests at least five strategies for improving company morale that get implemented.
- Achieve company objective of being listed as one of the top 100 companies to work for.
- Advise senior executives on low-cost morale-building strategies.

See also: Managing Performance, Personnel/Hiring/Retention

Human Resources and Personnel

Goals in this section can be used with employees in human resource departments or elsewhere involved in hiring and retention, including work-unit managers.

Hiring

- Screen job applicants so hiring managers are satisfied with the pool of applicants.
- Develop and implement an online job application system by year-end.
- Ensure that job applications are representative of the diversity of the local workforce.
- Develop strategies to increase qualified applications from members of minority groups by 10% next year.
- Keep recruitment costs within 10% of industry average.
- Fill all jobs within six weeks of initial job posting.
- Reduce the time needed to fill vacancies by 10% from previous year.
- Ensure that managers understand steps to follow to request additional staffing so they can do so with no errors or requests for clarification.

Staff Development

- With senior executives, prepare an annual staff development plan linked to the organization's strategic plan.
- Incorporate staff development planning in work-unit performance management process.
- Help employees find the most effective means of maintaining professional certification.
- Advise employees on recommended development activities that will increase their potential for promotion.
- Ensure that employees know about all product lines.

- Provide basic orientation for new employees that they rate as "above average" in surveys.
- Help managers provide specific job orientations with new hires to reduce time required to get new employees up to speed.
- Use acting status appointments to develop at least four promising managerial candidates per year.
- Maintain a database of training options for specific positions that at least 30% of employees consult in any given year.
- Develop a staff development plan that reflects the organization's skill needs for the upcoming year and incorporates input from executives, line managers, and employees.
- Advise on organizational development issues and refer managers to competent resources, to the satisfaction of the managers.
- Keep current and knowledgeable about current HR trends and laws by attending annual government briefings on HR law and attending one national HR conference per year.
- Maintain database of local trainers, including quality review information, so managers can arrange seminars without the intervention of HR.
- Reduce staff development costs while increasing staff development hours delivered by coordinating needs and solutions across the company and using economy of scale.
- Ensure that staff development planning is linked to the work-unit performance management process.
- Prepare cost benefit analysis of reducing classroom training and increasing use of alternative computer-mediated training methods by January 7, 20XX.

- Monitor completion rates of employees who use computer- and media-based instructional courses, and identify top reasons why some employees fail to complete.

Staff Retention/Promotion

- Ensure that at least 95% of promoted employees succeed, as reflected in yearly performance reviews.
- Maintain staff turnover ratio between 5% and 8% per year.
- Reduce new hire turnover to less than 10%.
- Reduce dismissals related to substance abuse to less than 3% of total dismissals.
- Reduce staff loss resulting from "insufficient challenge in job" by 10%.
- Conduct exit interviews for every employee and provide the HR manager a semiannual report on reasons for leaving.

Staff Satisfaction

- Conduct staff satisfaction surveys at least once every two years.
- Prepare recommendations to improve employee satisfaction, with at least two recommendations implemented each year.
- Use exit interview data to raise employee satisfaction levels.
- Chair employee satisfaction committee that suggests at least five strategies for improving company morale that get implemented.
- Achieve company objective of being listed as one of the top 100 companies to work for.

Conformance

- Ensure that hiring practices conform to Equal Employment Opportunity Commission requirements.

- Reduce substantiated discrimination complaints to zero.
- Advise the managers on legal interviewing techniques.
- Prepare and advise the managers for grievance hearings.
- Inform the CEO of potential illegal practices that put the company at risk.
- Procure expert legal advice on behalf of the company as needed.
- Complete human resources audit once every two years to determine conformance levels.
- Identify any illegal nonconformance to HR laws before external agencies do.

Policy Development/Communication

- Create a staff development policy that links staff development expenditures to the organization's needs.
- Communicate information about benefits package options in plain English, so most employees understand them.
- Consult with line managers on policy changes that affect them prior to rewriting policies.
- Write policies that managers can follow without asking additional questions.
- Prepare estimates of required staffing levels for next five years, to the satisfaction of the CFO.
- Research and report on potential outsourcing of HR functions, to the satisfaction of the CFO.
- Develop and communicate performance management policy to managers so that managers indicate they understand and can implement the policy.

Work-Unit Support

- Maintain job descriptions and update descriptions each year or as required by managers.

- Support managers in undertaking performance management so that managers complete 80% of appraisals on time.
- Provide employee assistance referrals to the satisfaction of managers and employees.
- Administer human resources database to maintain 98% uptime.
- Provide support to managers in handling layoff situations humanely.
- Develop a downsizing strategy that does not result in significant loss in productivity.
- Ensure that employees and managers complete forms provided by HR so that no more than 2% need revision.
- Respond to managers' requests for assistance within one working day.
- Help managers determine optimal staffing levels for work unit to maintain or increase effectiveness.
- Provide training to managers on conducting termination meetings safely and to satisfaction of the managers as indicated in feedback sheets.
- Provide at least three different forms from which managers can choose to track performance management.
- Provide legal interpretations to managers regarding personnel issues within two days of request and with at least 98% accuracy.
- Provide managers and employees with information about substance abuse rehabilitation resources available and increase the use of such resources to within 30% of the incidence of addiction in the population.

Compensation/Benefits
- Ensure that salary and benefits packages are competitive to attract top-quality candidates, according to unit managers.

- Ensure that compensation levels are within 10% of industry norms.
- Keep project salary costs for next year within 5% of estimates.
- Research and suggest options for new profit-sharing program.
- Ensure that no more than 5% of job offers are rejected due to inadequate salary and benefits.
- Maintain overall overtime levels at less than 4% of total payroll per month.
- Contribute to corporate team investigating health insurance options and write the final report for executive management.
- Identify best practices in providing day care and recommend to the board of directors a course of action that takes into account practicality and financial issues.

Labor Relations
- Reduce union labor actions to zero, while staying within financial guidelines.
- Reduce total grievances to 15 or fewer a year.
- Reduce total grievance proceedings losses to three per year.
- Reduce by 20% the time needed to come to labor agreements.
- Complete labor agreements for bargaining group by July 6 and stay within financial guidelines established by the CEO.
- Report bargaining deadlocks to the CFO within three hours of occurrence.

Other
- Provide clear guidance to systems personnel about HR requirements for personnel tracking system.

- Review and recommend possible options for HR management software to satisfaction of the CFO.
- Lead systems development initiative to develop an integrated HR management system to be completed by year-end.
- Ensure employees receive all tax documentation at least three weeks prior to government-set mandatory date.
- Attend local human resources association meetings and present on at least one topic each year.
- Make employee assistance referrals quickly enough to maximize outcomes.

See also: Managing Performance, Personnel/Hiring/Retention

Information Technology:
Hardware and Operations—Management

Goals in this section can be used with anyone involved in managing personnel with responsibilities for the selection, purchase, deployment, maintenance, and/or security of computer hardware, networks, and related job functions.

Project/Staff Management

- Ensure that 90% of projects are completed on time and require no rework.
- Ensure that all emergency calls are responded to within 20 minutes.
- Schedule operations staff to ensure 24-hour coverage in person or via pagers.
- Coordinate hardware and software teams to reduce unnecessary wait time for project implementation.
- Ensure that all hardware purchases delivered to customer are effective as indicated by minimum 85% of clients.
- Ensure that computer resources are available for all high-priority corporate initiatives.
- Identify key operational goals of other work units in conjunction with disaster recovery planning.
- Initiate and monitor yearly disaster recovery practice exercises to ensure all departments are following mandatory procedures and remedy if necessary.
- Negotiate computer operations chargeback rates with other department managers that are seen as fair by managers.
- Ensure that reports have skills and knowledge required to complete planned projects.

- Create schedules that anticipate staff absences and assign backup roles to staff on high-priority projects.

Purchasing and Maintenance
- Authorize purchases according to corporate priorities for current year.
- Prepare hardware procurement budgets that are approved without modification by the CFO.
- Ensure that total cost of purchased equipment for the year is within budget.
- Negotiate supplier contracts to balance cost versus quality of equipment.
- Review and approve cost estimates for capital expenditures prepared by direct reports.
- Contact each division manager at least once every two months to determine levels of satisfaction with supplied resources and to project/identify future needs.
- Ensure that other divisions use key suppliers to take advantage of negotiated discounts/cost savings.
- Ensure all hardware procurement follows corporate policies 100% of the time as determined by yearly audits.
- Develop rolling three year projections for computer hardware purchase that is within 10% of actual expenditures for each year.

Results Management
- Reduce reliance on paper files within total organization by creating document management system by June 20XX.
- Contribute to overall "white-collar" productivity improvement by 2% this year.
- Ensure that zero purchases are necessary that result from inadequate equipment maintenance.

- Reduce operations staff overtime by 15% this year.
- Improve job processing throughput by 10% without incurring additional costs.
- Ensure that 85% of users are satisfied that interactive response time is adequate.
- Prepare annual report for senior executives outlining major activities and costs and benefits of each of those activities.
- Eliminate data losses resulting from computer viruses.
- Consult with managers to reduce computer theft by 50% this year.
- Increase average lifespan before replacement of current desktop PCs by six months to reduce expenditures on replacements.

See also: Information Technology: Software—Management, Information Technology: Hardware and Operations

Information Technology: Hardware and Operations

Goals in this section can be used with anyone involved in the selection, purchase, deployment, maintenance, and security of computer hardware, networks, and related job functions.

Backups/Disaster Recovery

- Run daily backups as set out in backup schedule (no missed backups).
- Coordinate disaster recovery team dry runs at least twice a year.
- Ensure that disaster recovery process can be completed within two days of event with no loss of data.
- Inspect off-site disaster recovery center at least once a month to ensure operability.
- Ensure that all disaster recovery personnel are clear about their roles and functions in the event of a disaster.
- Deposit completed backups in company safe each day by 6 P.M.
- Send backup media to off-site backup center each day and verify receipt by 9 P.M.
- Maintain disaster recovery plan and communicate to all personnel required to implement the plan.
- Ensure that recovery plan reflects corporate and business priorities.
- Ensure that security/recovery procedures do not negatively impact business functions.

Customer Support

- Acknowledge requests for hardware repairs/maintenance within one hour of receipt when received on a workday, or within 36 hours if not.

- Inform customers of planned computer outages at least one working day prior to outage.
- Provide basic training to customers on accessing and using computer network.
- Set up accounts for users within three hours of receiving request.
- Notify job/process owners when jobs are going to be delayed more than one hour.
- Collect information from computer users at least once a year on possible enhancements to the network.
- Collect information from departmental managers regarding their projections for both hardware and software needs for the upcoming year at least two months before compiling summary report for executives.
- Communicate regarding departmental manager requests for new hardware within one working day to acknowledge receipt, and within one week to advise on decision making about request.

Data and Hardware Security

- Monitor networks and report any attempts at unauthorized system access to security within 24 hours of attempt.
- Develop and implement corporate strategy for reducing junk e-mail by 50% by December 20XX.
- Reduce incidence of virus infection on corporate computers to no more than one per year.
- Advise users on safe computing practices to prevent virus infections.
- Ensure that all systems passwords for all users are at least nine alphanumeric characters and implement automated system to ongoing conformance by April 20XX.

- Develop and communicate procedures to ensure that each computer can be accessed by computer owner only.
- Secure network servers so only authorized personnel have physical access.
- Carry out security audits without disrupting regular business processes according to department managers.
- Reduce theft of computer equipment within company to less than $1,000 per year.
- With human resources, develop policy on acceptable use of computer resources by December 20XX.
- Complete monthly computer/Internet access audits to identify any possible violations of acceptable use policy.

Maintenance and Operations

- Ensure that unplanned network downtime is limited to no more than once every two months.
- Schedule all planned downtime to occur after regular workday.
- Maintain existing desktop PCs so no employee is without computer access for more than one working day.
- Notify systems staff within one hour of failure of scheduled computer runs.
- Prioritize requests for computer maintenance to reflect relative business-case priorities.
- Reduce job reruns due to operator error to no more than one per week.
- Monitor and maintain computing environment so zero shutdowns are required per month due to temperature or other environmental issues.
- Participate in and advise energy management group on possible strategies to reduce computer-related energy requirements.

- Maintain network cables and wiring so there is no more than one network problem per two months attributable to cabling.
- Report computer usage statistics to each departmental manager within 10 days of end of each month.
- Reduce user complaints about delays or slowdowns on network to no more than one per month.
- Monitor and report on corporate use of Internet and recommend best strategies to maintain effective high-speed access for users.

New Equipment
- Help managers prepare a cost-benefit analysis for the purchase of new hardware that proves to be accurate within 10% of actual results.
- Prioritize requests for new equipment to reflect relative business-case priorities.
- Ensure that new equipment works properly when made available to users.
- Review cost-benefit analyses, make recommendations, and submit to the CFO so it takes no more than one month to complete new equipment request review.
- Anticipate needs for new equipment and budget for it so no business process is negatively impacted by outdated or nonworking equipment.
- Prepare and submit budget for new equipment acquisitions to division manager no later than September 30 of each year.
- Explain reasons why request for new equipment has been postponed or denied, to satisfaction of requesting manager.
- Ensure that all equipment purchased is compatible with existing software and hardware 100% of the time.

- Ensure that all new hardware is operational within seven days of receipt or in accordance with agreed-upon schedule.

See also: Information Technology: Hardware and Operations—Management, Information Technology: Software

Information Technology: Software—Management

Goals in this section can be used with anyone involved in leading, managing, or supervising individual staff or teams involved in developing, programming, testing, and deploying software systems and solutions.

Communication/Training

- Select and groom an individual to perform the supervisory role so that supervisor's absence is "seamless."

- Provide training for new data entry clerks based on individual learning style so that each new clerk is fully functional within one month of hire.

- Coach and mentor junior analysts so that more subject matter experts are available for work assignments.

- Ensure that line managers understand sign-off procedures so zero changes need to be made to specs after sign-off date.

- Ensure that complete documentation for all software projects is available to clients.

- Advise and support line managers so software solutions increase productivity by a minimum of 10%.

- Coordinate training of end users so all staff are trained and productive within two weeks after system goes online.

Productivity

- Develop strategy to improve the data entry process so that overtime is eliminated.

- Coordinate work with other IT managers so no delays result from lack of communication.

- Chair analyst/programmer meetings so that all agenda items are completed each meeting.

- Reduce average system development life cycle by a minimum of 10% by December 20XX.
- Advise the CFO on relative merits of outsourcing vs. in-house development, to the satisfaction of the CFO.
- Coordinate project personnel to eliminate duplicate effort.
- Reduce rework by 20%.
- Create data quality standards that reflect client needs by June 20.
- Make sure that systems do what they are expected to do, according to clients.

Project Management

- Assign data entry special assignments to appropriate personnel so that the data is entered accurately and within the specified time.
- Maintain the expected 80-to-20 supervisor ratio by using 20% of the week performing data entry tasks and 80% of the week performing supervisory tasks.
- Inform data entry clerks of possible changes to completion times of assignments so that they can manage their work and home life accordingly.
- Schedule and manage on-call staff so emergency pages are answered within 20 minutes.
- Prioritize incoming line manager requests according to overall company priorities.
- Ensure that 90% of all software development projects are completed no more than two weeks late.
- Ensure that all new systems developed are ISO 9000 compliant.

See also: Information Technology: Hardware and Operations—Management, Information Technology: Software

Information Technology: Software

Goals in this section can be used with anyone involved in developing, programming, testing, and deploying software systems and solutions and anyone involved with data entry.

Data Entry

- Input data with a speed of 8,000-plus keystrokes per hour.
- Input data with an accuracy rate of 98% or better.
- Edit input prior to data entry so that data is accepted into system with a 95% success rate.
- Recognize and resolve data issues within 24 hours of discovery.
- Proofread coworkers' inputted data and identify all errors.
- Work overtime at least two hours per week.
- Inform supervisor of possible changes to completion times of assignments so that client expectations and department work schedules can be managed accordingly.

Business Systems Analysis

- Identify and solve problems using department standard problem-solving process before problems can affect the clients.
- Identify alternative solutions to a business problem or opportunity, recommend a solution, and allow client to select the best one.
- Communicate with all groups of people equally well, knowing when to provide management summary information and when to provide detailed information, so that each group has the information required to make its business decisions.

- Document business and systems requirements appropriately for each group of people so that the programmer can code the solution and the clients can understand what is being delivered and an appropriate test strategy can be applied.
- Design and deliver presentations to clients with one week's notice or less and to the satisfaction of the clients.
- Train end users so that they can use new software within an acceptable time, as defined by the end users.
- Work productively with all team members within each phase of the system development life cycle so that the system or solution is delivered accurately and on time.
- Review vendor software to determine its fit for use within the system.

Programming

- Use department standard coding techniques so that code delivered is easily maintained and upgraded as required.
- Identify alternative coding solutions and recommend a solution to more junior programmers to allow them to acquire systems and business knowledge.
- Document coding and systems solutions appropriately so that solutions to future problems or upgrades can be implemented easily and in a timely manner.
- Apply knowledge of clients' needs and priorities so systems changes or upgrades can be proactive rather than reactive, decreasing time to market.
- Provide feedback on team programmers' coding solutions; suggest better coding when appropriate.
- Document coding changes within each program so as to keep a good and updated history of program changes, reducing the time to market when program changes or upgrades are required.

- Design technical tools for department use that reduces the time required to perform the "business as usual" tasks by 10%.
- Review vendor software to determine its fit for use within the system.
- Deliver program code to production at least 98% bug-free.
- Create 100 lines of program code per day.
- Provide programming effort estimates within 10% of actuals to facilitate the scheduling of project tasks.

Testing

- Identify major system components to facilitate the estimation of time required to test system upgrade or single change.
- Analyze software defects to detect patterns that help discern system problems so that system solutions can be implemented in a timely manner.
- Apply the various test types appropriate to each phase of the system development life cycle.
- Input appropriate test data with which to test the system with fewer than five entry errors.
- Test system with sufficient detail so that the system does not have any major problems when it is implemented.
- Attend to detail so that each system defect is recorded and retested until it is resolved.
- Categorize each system defect so that "showstoppers" are addressed before minor problems.
- Document results so that testing progress can be determined in regard to timeliness, number of defects found, number of defects resolved, number of defects retested, etc.

System Deployment

- Contact most appropriate personnel for problem resolution during implementation.

- Analyze implementation problems to detect patterns that help discern solutions so that system can be implemented on time.

- Understand and apply the company's best practices regarding implementation strategies.

- Recognize and point out potential problems when developers develop their implementation plan.

- Schedule the company's various system changes and upgrades.

System Support (Help Desk)

- Respond to each client within 15 minutes of receiving a description of the problem.

- Resolve the problem within 24 hours of client's initial contact.

- Provide department- or company-wide messages providing details of a current problem when required.

- Communicate courteously to clients who are experiencing problems, to the satisfaction of the clients.

- Escalate the problem as required but only when necessary.

- Provide resolution instructions to each client in writing, via voice mail, or over the phone, according to the client's preference.

- Follow up with client 48 hours after resolving the problem.

- Document a history of each problem logged and forward to supervisor each week.

See also: Information Technology: Hardware and Operations, Information Technology: Software—Management

Internet/Intranet Related

The Internet (general access) and the intranet (internal access only) have become major tools for businesses whether it be as a way of communicating via e-mail with customers and between employees, or as methods to market, support customers, and monitor brands and reputation. Here you will find goals related to positions that are involved in the development, maintenance, and use of Internet and intranet resources.

Community Development and Customer Support

- Identify open source alternatives to commercial community forum software and provide recommendations on procurement of software for customer support forum according to criteria established.

- Ensure all communication methods with customers include reference to online support forum (integrated communication strategy) and partner with other departments to achieve.

- Arrange to staff the support community so there is never more than a three-hour gap in moderating and responding to help requests.

- Interact with expert customers to encourage them to actively participate on a daily or semi-daily basis to help others.

- Ensure spam posts are eliminated or are removed within three hours of posting.

- Market/communicate about company's community support forums by messaging on Twitter, Facebook, and LinkedIn at least once a week.

- Monitor social media platforms (Twitter, LinkedIn) to identify people having difficulties with service and to proactively guide them to the community support forums.

Content Development and Blogging

- Write relevant articles for corporate blog of at least 350 words on topics identified in editorial schedule.
- Increase blog visitor comments/interactions by 25% over the next six months.
- Identify and implement new features for the blog to increase average time spent on blog by one minute per visitor.
- Develop content consistent with search engine optimization to increase percentage of visitors coming from Google and Bing to 40% of total visits.
- Increase percentage of return visitors from average of 12% of total traffic to 20% of total traffic without reducing total visits.
- Increase total page views per visitor by 40% by June 15, 20XX.

Hardware Management

- Determine hardware configuration that is most economical and efficient to use to host corporate blog and prepare purchasing recommendations.
- Maintain Web/blog server uptime at 99.9% except for monthly scheduled maintenance.
- Maintain server security by applying server software patches within 12 hours of release.
- Monitor server loads and ensure no unplanned downtime as a result of increased server requirements.
- Upgrade physical server before response time degrades or visitors are inconvenienced due to crashes.

- Make leasing arrangements for co-located servers, and ensure vendor can address hardware issues 24/7 if required.

Intranet Content Manager

- Develop and maintain customer service knowledge base so it contains all up-to-date solutions to top 200 customer questions.
- Arrange for and follow up to make sure CEO contributes agreed upon monthly message for posting on intranet.
- Train designated departmental contributors so they can use content management system to share their weekly hints and tips posts with other employees.
- Develop engaging content so employees develop habit of checking into intranet for news at least once every week.
- Create RSS feeds so each employee will receive automatic and real-time updates of any new information posted on intranet.
- "Market" intranet content to managers and employees to increase awareness and usage as problem-solving tool.
- Prepare annual usage report along with recommendations for improving the intranet to the chief information officer by December 1, 20XX, to satisfaction of the CIO.
- Supervise creation of a mobile version of company intranet so it is usable by employees away from the office who use smart phones, by April 2012.
- Respond to employee questions, offers to contribute, and comments within one working day of receipt of communication.

Social Media Involvement

- With heads of marketing and sales, develop a three-year strategic plan to utilize the major social media platforms to increase new sales and improve customer service, by July 10, 20XX.

- Develop policy for employee use of Internet/social media that is approved by both head of HR and legal counsel by July 9, 20XX.
- Ensure social media use policy is re-examined each year and revised to reflect any changes in laws or company needs.
- Identify and enlist key contact people to function as communication hubs for Facebook, Twitter, and LinkedIn.
- Make recommendations regarding possible involvement on YouTube that takes into account demographics and limited resources by April 2, 20XX.
- Monitor mention of brands across all major social networks to develop business intelligence about how to create improved perception of products, and do executive summaries to go to head of HR, marketing, corporate communications, and sales by July 5, 20XX.
- Increase number of "friends"/"fans" on Facebook to the 3,000 mark by [date].
- Using discount "coupons" on Twitter, demonstrate capability to sell a minimum of 100 units during the test phase of first Twitter-based campaign.
- Monitor comments and input on company's Facebook account/fan page and identify one comment each week as "comment of the week;" commenter to receive a prize of no more than $30 in value and no less than $20.
- Ensure comments made about the company or brand, either negative or positive, on Twitter are responded to within 24 hours during the week.
- As representative of the company, develop a personal presence on LinkedIn by participating in relevant groups at least three times a week in a non-sales-oriented way (be visible).

Web Design, Development, Webmastering, and Web Maintenance

- Engage graphic artist to consult on the new modified layout for website, and submit ideas for final approval to VP of marketing.

- Update website software used to implement latest security patches and features within 24 hours of them being released.

- Develop a new navigation structure and system to reduce complaints from visitors about difficulty finding things on website to zero.

- On a yearly basis, examine website and user statistics plus competitor sites to determine whether to update and modernize the website as standards change and evolve.

- Coordinate content contributors so new content is added on a weekly basis.

- Hire expertise in search engine optimization with the goal of increasing our ranking on top-ten targeted key words so company appears on the first page of search results on Bing and Google.

- Incorporate more interactive components into static website and increase visitor comments to company or about content by 20% in the next year.

- Consult with department heads to determine what each of their messages should be as presented to visitors to the website, write the copy, and have each department head sign off.

- Ensure that links to external sites are operating and valid.

- Monitor shopping cart system to ensure it is operating properly (uptime) 99.5% of time.

- Identify times when visits and Web-based sales are lowest and schedule planned maintenance for those windows to minimize sales losses.
- User-test any new releases of scripts and software prior to them going into production, with zero defects that negatively impact on Web-based sales.
- Maintain Web privacy policy and revise on a yearly basis as required by industry changes and trends.
- Respond to e-mail "to Webmaster" within one working day.
- For interactive sections of the website, ensure spam and inappropriate messages containing obscenities or material unsuitable for a business site are removed within three hours of appearing.

Mechanical Repair and Trades

Goals in this section can be used for employees directly involved in the repair of machinery of various sorts and trades like plumbing, carpentry, auto mechanics, and welding.

Customer Communication

- Provide an estimate to the customer within the time span agreed upon.
- Inform the customer of any other mechanical problems found during repair.
- Explain clearly the consequences of not repairing a mechanical problem.
- Provide advice to the customer on whether a repair is worth doing.
- Notify the customer when the repair is completed.
- Contact each customer one week after repair to determine his or her satisfaction with the repair.
- Present a clear, itemized bill upon conclusion of repairs that comes within 10% of the estimate.
- Notify the client if arriving more than 10 minutes late.
- Inform the client of options regarding repair parts and the merits of each so he or she can make an informed choice.

Diagnosis and Quality of Work

- Diagnose problems accurately at least 95% of the time.
- Ensure that repairs do not have to be redone within one year.
- Ensure that repairs outlast warranty on repairs in at least 95% of cases.
- Attend appropriate training courses each year to refresh diagnostic skills and learn about changes in new models.

- Ensure that all repair work complies with all relevant safety guidelines.
- Ensure that no repairs fail inspection by third-party safety inspectors.
- Maintain area of repair so no injuries occur while repair is ongoing.
- Post appropriate signage to guide people away from repair area.
- Make repairs so that zero property damage occurs as a result of the poor quality of any repair.
- Meet customer needs so that 90% of customers are satisfied, as determined through follow-up calls.
- Test all repairs before leaving to ensure that they actually solve the problem.

Speed of Repair
- Complete every repair within the specified "book time" for that kind of repair 95% of the time.
- Ensure that no more than 5% of repairs are delayed due to lack of parts or tools.
- Arrive for every repair visit with all necessary tools and parts.
- Make every effort to minimize the amount of time the machinery is unavailable for customer use.

Work Planning and Estimating
- Plan projects so that unproductive downtime attributable to poor planning is eliminated.
- Provide accurate, fair, and honest estimates.
- Schedule field repairs to reduce mileage/transportation costs by 10%.
- Plan so arrival at repair site is within 10 minutes of time promised.

- Schedule the shutdown of machinery for repair to have the least possible impact on the customer's business and/or life.
- Maximize billing hours through effective work planning.
- Maintain billable hours at an average of 30 hours per week level.

See also: Customer Service and Support

Goals in this section can be used with management and supervisory staff involved in supervising maintenance, repair, and cleaning activities related to the physical space and equipment in the workplace.

Cleaning

- Ensure that department managers make no more than one complaint per month about cleaning not being completed properly.
- Contract with outside cleaning agencies to provide required cleaning services within allocated cleaning budget.
- Schedule cleaning staff to minimize overtime and ensure that all required cleaning is done on time.
- Do spot checks of premises at least once a day to ensure cleanliness.
- Review cleaning logs to make sure washrooms are cleaned on schedule.
- Review customer feedback forms and alter cleaning schedules to increase "cleanliness" rating by 20%.
- Maintain cleaning supplies inventory to ensure zero need for employees to make special purchases due to shortages.
- Ensure that all volatile cleaning materials are kept secure, with access restricted to cleaning staff.
- Work with cleaning staff to research and recommend better cleaning products.

Plant Maintenance

- Ensure that plant downtime related to emergency repairs totals no more than three hours per month.

- Develop maintenance schedules for major equipment that result in a 10% reduction of total downtime due to equipment failures.
- Prioritize requests for maintenance, according to the potential impact on safety and productivity.
- Ensure that overall response time for requests for maintenance is within company requirements and specifications.
- Meet regularly with supervisors and line managers to identify ways the maintenance unit can provide better service to them.
- Ensure that unplanned emergency purchases constitute no more than 10% of the physical plant maintenance budget each year.
- Arrange for normal elevator maintenance to occur outside of peak work hours.
- Help the VP operations identify major equipment replacements that will be necessary within next two years.
- Solicit from equipment users at least one maintenance improvement strategy to reduce unplanned failures.
- Review problem-reporting procedures and improve as necessary.

Safety

- Chair workplace safety and health committee during 20XX.
- Ensure that all maintenance employees understand and follow emergency procedures.
- Arrange for immediate emergency repair of critical emergency systems within one hour of being notified.
- Assign and train staff in roles in emergency shutdown and evacuation situations.
- Coordinate third-party inspections of critical physical plant machinery (boilers, elevators) to comply with government certification requirements.

- Develop and implement a maintenance strategy to reduce customer injuries requiring medical attention to zero in the upcoming year.
- Review and stay current on government workplace safety and health regulations.
- Ensure that maintenance employees report and remedy violations of government guidelines before they are identified by outside inspectors.

See also: Workplace Health and Safety—Management

Physical Plant Maintenance

Goals in this section can be used with employees involved in any maintenance, repair, and cleaning activities related to the physical space and equipment in the workplace.

Cleaning

■ Inspect washrooms at least once an hour and identify cleaning needs.

■ Ensure that customers rate "cleanliness of establishment" as at least "very good."

■ Complete cleaning logs with no errors.

■ Complete end-of-shift cleanup so employees on the following shift do not complain about tasks not completed.

■ Use appropriate cleaning solutions and products for job, according to supervisor.

■ Inform supervisor of upcoming shortages of cleaning supplies so no shortage interferes with maintenance.

■ Respond to requests for aisle cleanup within 10 minutes and complete the cleanup within 20 minutes.

■ Ensure that doorways into facility are clear of ice and snow or other impediments to customers.

■ Place cleaning equipment so it does not block entryways for more than five minutes at a time during cleaning.

■ Clean windows in public view to maintain clear, unobstructed vision and clean appearance.

■ Maintain cleaning equipment inventory so all items are easily accessible and access to the items is not blocked.

■ Process empty cleaning materials containers in prescribed and safe way.

Plant Maintenance

- Respond to emergency physical plant situations within 20 minutes of notification.

- Shut down the heating system in emergency situations according to manufacturer's shutdown instructions.

- Eliminate your own maintenance errors that affect plant productivity.

- Eliminate injuries to employees resulting from your own errors in maintaining assigned equipment.

- Inform supervisor of the progress of every repair so he or she can communicate effectively with plant supervisors as needed.

- Carry out preventative maintenance for assigned machines and as set out in manufacturers' guidelines.

- Identify probable causes of potential failure of major equipment and notify manager for preventive repair and replacement so catastrophic failure of business-critical equipment stays at zero.

- Maintain maintenance and repair logs for all major physical plant machinery.

- Develop and maintain positive relationships with outside repair and maintenance personnel.

Safety

- Notify management and HAZMAT team of any potential hazardous substance spills within 10 minutes of identifying them.

- Spot and remove any items out of place that may constitute safety hazards.

- Place warning signs when cleaning floors so there are zero customer accidents related to improper signage.

- Eliminate all occurrences of spillage of hazardous material as a result of your own handling errors.

- Participate and contribute to workplace safety and health committee.
- Participate in monthly checks and inspections of all safety equipment including fire alarms, smoke detectors, and carbon monoxide detectors.

See also: Workplace Health and Safety

Production/Manufacturing

Goals in this section can be used for those directly involved in manufacturing or producing physical items.

Quantity

- Produce at least 12 widgets per shift.
- Ensure that the assembly line is not slowed down or shut down because of your work more than once a month.
- Help others achieve their production quotas.
- Show progressive increases in output over next six months.
- Manage supplies so output is not reduced due to lack of parts.
- Maintain your output per shift within ±10% of your average output each month.
- Identify barriers to increased output and work with management to eliminate.
- Work with the product design team to develop new products that are easy to assemble quickly.
- Use assembly techniques that do not slow down the work of others.
- Balance quantity and quality of output to maximize cost-effectiveness.
- Work safely so no line shutdown is required due to any unsafe work procedures on your part.
- Ask for help when your processing speed becomes an impediment to output.
- Proactively seek out and learn new practices and procedures to increase your output.
- Maintain your equipment so there are zero instances of loss of output due to improper tool maintenance.

Quality

- Ensure that no more than 2% of the items you produce are rejected for quality reasons.
- Ensure that no more than 4% of the items you produce require rework.
- Contribute to developing an overall strategy to reduce rework.
- Ensure that 98% of the items you produce meet quality standards.
- Contribute to work-unit establishment of quality standards for products.
- Identify all products received that do not meet standards and return them to the previous station.
- Document any quality problems for use in future troubleshooting.
- Apply statistical process control tools to identify the root causes of quality problems.
- Lead the quality improvement team.
- Stop the assembly line quickly whenever poor quality outputs reach your station.

Safety and Environment

- Follow all safety procedures during assembly 100% of the time.
- Leave the work station clean and functional at the end of the shift.
- Keep the work station free of clutter that may constitute a safety hazard for others.
- Return all tools to their proper places when not in use.
- Report all equipment problems to maintenance as soon as possible, to reduce downtime.

- Wear and use all safety equipment 100% of the time when on the floor.
- Receive zero reprimands for safety violations.
- Encourage coworkers to work safely and abide by safety procedures.

See also: Work Outputs and Productivity

Retail/Merchandising—Management

Goals in this section can be used with anyone working in the retail sector who supervises or manages employees.

Customer Service

■ Handle customer complaints so no more than one per month go to head office.

■ Talk with at least five customers per day to assess customer satisfaction.

■ Ensure that average customer checkout time is less than four minutes.

■ Provide customer service improvement suggestions to head office at least twice yearly.

■ Ensure that floor workers have sufficient product knowledge to respond to customer inquiries effectively.

Scheduling/Staffing

■ Reduce overtime 10% by hiring temporary and/or backup staff.

■ Reduce staff absenteeism to less than 1% of total days worked in store.

■ Ensure that all employees have adequate product knowledge, as indicated by customer feedback.

■ Ensure that all employees are properly certified as required.

■ Conform to staffing guidelines from the head office.

■ Identify employees who are candidates for promotion within next year and forward the information to human resources.

■ Develop and implement an employee-of-the-month system so that 80% of the employees surveyed find it constructive.

Store Management

- Reduce shrinkage by 2% per month from last year's figures.

- Completely eliminate health code violations in 2011.

- Ensure that the store follows the merchandising requirements of the company.

- Ensure that the store meets its revenue and budget targets for each month.

- Report anticipated monthly revenue shortfalls to head office by the 15th of each month.

- Maintain rating of at least 4 out of 5 from corporate mystery shoppers.

- Forecast customer demand for stock within 10% of actuals.

- Order stock to accommodate customer demand.

- Meet monthly projections of gross profit as compared with comparable stores.

See also: Customer Service and Support—Management, Financial, Security—Management, Food Preparation—Management, Retail/Merchandising

Retail/Merchandising

Goals in this section can be used with employees working in the retail sector at all levels of an organization, but particularly in retail locations.

Checkout/Cash Register

- Process 90% of customers within five minutes.
- Promote special offers to customers when appropriate to circumstances.
- Direct customers to proper aisle for desired products, without help.
- Balance the cash register and come within $1 98% of the time.
- Make sure that cash register discrepancies never exceed $10 per shift.
- Engage in friendly conversation with customers without sacrificing speed of scanning or otherwise entering items.
- Manage checkout lines and direct customers to other, faster lines.
- Process returns and refunds properly and without help from supervisor.
- Input items with no more than 1% error in amounts.
- Calculate change due to customers, both with and without machines.
- Wrap/package customer goods with no more than 2% reported damage.

Customer Service

- Fit customers with the proper size to the satisfaction of the customers.
- Offer the customers value-added services every time (e.g., parcel carryout).

- Teach customers about new features in store, as appropriate.
- Offer corporate credit cards to all customers, with a sign-up rate of at least 1%.
- Relay customer complaints to the manager at the end of each day.
- Smile and greet customers, to the satisfaction of the supervisor.
- Acknowledge customers waiting for service.

Retail Environment
- Place impulse buying items at checkout.
- Maintain the lights so no more than 2% are inoperative at any given time.
- Respond to emergency cleanup requests within four minutes of request.
- Ensure that all shelves under your control are neat and orderly by the end of each shift.
- Ensure that 98% of stock have UPCs and pricing codes in place at any given time.
- Keep aisles clear and free from debris.
- Maintain area so 95% of products are in proper locations.
- Keep food sampling tables clean and sanitary; empty garbage pails when they become three-quarters full.
- Rotate special feature displays around the store each week.
- Provide cooking instructions and recipes when customers ask for them.
- Ensure that seasonal displays are timely and removed immediately after the seasonal event.
- Check featured item displays at beginning of each shift to ensure that they are in place and in good condition.

Stock/Inventory

- Ensure that inventory on hand is sufficient to meet customer demand for sales items.
- Reduce issuing of rain checks by 20% in any given month.
- Ensure expired products are removed from display.
- Reduce product wastage by 10%.
- Ensure that departmental shrinkage is below store average.
- Remove all damaged or unsealable merchandise from displays.
- Keep old product in front of new product.
- Operate stocking machines, forklifts, and ladders safely in accordance with operating procedures.
- Follow stock security procedures each time valuable items are accessed.
- Dispose of spoiled produce in accordance with procedures outlined in job aid.
- Ensure that 90% of high-demand items are safely accessible to all customers.
- Inform the manager of any inventory arriving damaged or spoiled within three hours of arrival.
- Ensure that all items are dated accurately.
- Report to the designated manager any discrepancies between inventory received and inventory expected as soon as you observe them.
- Ensure that the time lag between product being received at the loading dock and appearing on the shelves in saleable condition is no greater than three hours.
- Put new items in the storage area as soon as they arrive so sales staff can access them easily.

See also: Customer Service and Support, Financial, Food Preparation, Retail/Merchandising—Management, Security

Sales and Business Development—Management

Goals in this section can be used with people supervising or managing sales functions in organizations.

Generating New Sales/Customers

- Improve sales to 18–24 demographic by 5%.
- Reduce cost per customer acquisition to $25.
- Coach sales staff in improving initial approaches to customers.
- Monitor cold calls to potential customers and provide feedback to staff.
- Coordinate conference presentations to generate a minimum of 10 new customers per appearance.
- Promote new products through media appearances at least six times this year.
- Conclude at least one new distributor agreement involving at least $1,000,000 in sales.

Managing Current Sales/Customer Relations

- Increase average expenditure per visit by 10% across the department.
- Ensure delivery of sold products on schedule 97% of the time across the department.
- Contact all key accounts at least once every month to obtain feedback and offer help.
- Retain at least 95% of current distributors.

Sales Strategy Development

- Identify major reasons why sales aren't closed and suggest strategies to improve close ratio.

- Collect, summarize, and analyze customer input; generate suggestions for new products and submit them annually to the product director.
- Provide possible new product ideas to the director of product development, based on feedback from customers.
- Ensure that sales promotions result in 1:1.5 payback ratio.

Sales Training/Communication

- Conduct sales training seminars for subordinates at least once every two months.
- Develop strategy for sharing successful selling techniques.
- Diagnose and address skill gaps in supervised sales staff.
- Develop a modular training program for newly hired salespeople.
- Coordinate with marketing and production to prepare sales staff for new product rollout.
- Ensure that sales materials and brochures are available to sales staff when required.
- Provide sales projections to production to ensure that all orders can be filled on time.
- Provide monthly sales reports to VP of sales no later than 5th of next month.
- Notify VP of sales of anticipated sales shortfalls no later than 15th of sales month.
- Forecast monthly sales projections that are no more than ±12% off actuals.

See also: Customer Service and Support—Management, Retail/Merchandising—Management

Sales and Business Development

Goals in this section can be used with employees in sales positions or supervising sales staff.

Managing Current Sales/Customers

- Maintain personal customer retention ratio at 95% or higher.
- Cross-sell additional products to increase value of secondary purchases to $10,000 per month.
- Increase average expenditure per client transaction to $200.
- Increase average expenditure per visit by 10%.
- Maintain monthly contact with customers spending more than $500/month for upselling purposes.
- Achieve or exceed sales quotas on monthly basis.
- Increase sales to current large accounts (> $50K annually) by 20%.
- Generate at least two customer referrals a month from current customers.

Generating New Sales/Customers

- Improve sales to 18–24 demographic by 5%.
- Close sales for 20% of new leads provided.
- Reduce cost per customer acquisition to $25.
- Reduce time per customer acquisition to one hour (face-to-face or phone).
- Promote new product/service X so it constitutes 15% of personal sales.
- Bring in one mega-account worth sales of $1,000,000.
- Reduce reliance on small account sales (< $10K per annum) by concentrating on developing large accounts.
- Introduce product/service X to three new markets.

Sales-Related Customer Relations

- Provide estimates to customers that are within 5% of customer cost.
- Provide estimates for project conclusion accurate within five days.
- Retain customers so that no more than five per year ask to be transferred to another sales rep.
- Maintain overall rating by customers of at least "good" on survey instrument.
- Be organized enough to meet customer contact commitments at least 95% of the time.
- Project a professional image to potential customers during sales presentations.
- Respond to sales inquiries within three hours.
- Ensure on-schedule delivery of sold product 97% of the time.

Sales Strategy Development

- Identify major reasons why sales aren't closed and suggest strategies to improve close ratio.
- Identify customer issues/barriers to sales and participate in sales strategy development team.
- Collect, summarize, and analyze customer input; generate suggestions for new products and submit them annually to the product director.
- Work with marketing/advertising to develop new advertising strategies based on your understanding of your customers.
- As part of total sales team, contribute to sales increases of a minimum of 5% for each salesperson on team.
- Develop a modular training program for newly hired salespeople.

- Collect customer comments and pass them along to marketing.

Sales Training

- Train peers in best practices in sales.
- Share sales techniques with peers at monthly sales meetings.
- Conduct sales training seminars for subordinates at least once every two months.
- Develop a strategy for sharing successful selling techniques.
- Diagnose and address skill gaps in supervised sales staff.
- As product expert, train other sales staff to sell new product/service X.
- Train other staff so their sales of new product constitute 15% of total sales.

See also: Customer Service and Support, Retail/Merchandising

Security—Management

Goals in this section can be used with anyone in supervisory or management positions in departments responsible for the security of people, data, products, and physical environment.

Communication

- Coordinate work with police and other agencies to the satisfaction of those agencies.
- Ensure that the emergency procedures manual is available and accessible to all employees.
- Provide employee assistance program information to victims within 10 hours of incident.
- Contact the employee assistance director within 24 hours of any violent incident, to arrange appropriate counseling available.
- Develop and communicate a disaster evacuation plan.
- Deliver refresher courses to security staff at least once a year.
- Provide information to employees about drug-testing procedures, to the satisfaction of employees.
- Write a yearly report summarizing security statistics and making recommendations to the CEO about required security upgrades.
- Research and report on the need for personal security devices to be furnished to employees.

Compliance

- Help line managers schedule so there are always at least two staff members in the store after dark.
- Ensure that all security-related policies conform to federal, state, and local laws and requirements.

- Ensure that all drug-screening programs are consistent with existing human rights legislation (zero court-upheld challenges).
- Respond to every customer complaint about security staff within one working day.

Improvement

- Reduce the cost of vandalism to less than $1,000 per year.
- Develop and implement at least two new theft-prevention techniques per year.
- Reduce incidents of physical violence against staff by 15% in 20XX.
- Reduce drug test positives by 10% in the upcoming year.

Supervision and Training

- Schedule mobile patrols so each floor is checked at least once per hour.
- Ensure that all fixed-post security employees are alert (zero reports of inattentive security staff from building occupants).
- Ensure that main desk security employees use the visitor-tracking system as indicated in the security manual.
- Ensure that all security staff have, wear, and use appropriate uniforms and identification badges at all times.
- Help all security staff members procure and maintain "Certified Protection Professional" status.

Theft

- Implement an employee-monitoring strategy in high-risk areas.
- Maintain theft levels at less than 1% of total inventory.
- Work with managers in high-theft departments to reduce theft in those departments by 20% this year.

- Develop and implement key-tracking system to ensure that no unauthorized personnel have access to locked spaces.

See also: Security, Workplace Health and Safety

Security

Goals in this section can be used with employees responsible for security in the workplace, including those charged with the security of physical goods and facilities and the security and safety of people in the work environment.

Communication and Training

- Ensure that all employees understand emergency procedures for dealing with violent situations.
- Ensure that all employees are trained in techniques for preventing theft and violence.
- Ensure that all employees are trained and able to use observation and incident-reporting tools properly.
- Compile monthly incident reports and forward to head office before 15th of each month.
- Identify employee skill deficits that may negatively affect safety and security.
- Coordinate work with police and other agencies to the satisfaction of those agencies.

Compliance

- Follow cash-handling procedures as per company procedures.
- Schedule so there are always at least two staff members in the store after dark.
- Complete and pass training prescribed for security personnel each year.
- Maintain certification in CPR and other first-aid techniques.
- With police, conduct annual safety audit inspections.
- Comply with policies governing professional appearance and conduct as specified by the employer.

Enforcement

- Use least possible force in dealing with shoplifters: no physical injuries that require hospitalization.
- Maintain your own fitness levels to company standards as measured each year.
- Reduce nonvalid shoplifting-related customer stops to less than 5% of total stops.
- Maintain validated customer complaints about enforcement practices to an average of less than one per month.
- Respond to staff requests for assistance within two minutes.
- Provide accurate follow-up and incident documentation promptly.
- Use verbal self-defense techniques to reduce the need for force, to the satisfaction of the supervisor.
- Involve or refer to law enforcement officers as needed and in accordance with company policy.
- Apply standard accident and criminal investigation techniques in each situation.
- Gather evidence and prepare cases successfully for filing complaints, as verified by courts and the police.
- Use proper legal techniques for searching suspects.
- Use proper procedures for search and seizure, as verified by police.
- Use vehicle safely for patrol and pursuit, with no accidents in which the police determine the security employee to be at fault.
- Interview witnesses using proper questioning techniques within the bounds of legality.
- Secure and monitor prisoners according to police guidelines.

- Receive zero validated serious complaints from employees or customers.
- Demonstrate proper weapons safety procedures at all times.

Improvement
- Reduce the cost of vandalism to less than $1,000 per year.
- Develop and implement at least two new theft-prevention techniques per year.
- Reduce physical violence incidents aimed at staff by 15% in 20XX.

Theft
- Implement an employee-monitoring strategy in high-risk areas.
- Maintain theft levels at less than 1% of total inventory.
- Ensure that the electronic theft prevention system is working properly.
- Keep items identified as high-theft targets in secure cases until sold.

Personal Security
- Conduct an annual safety audit to identify potentially risky personal security habits.
- Conduct background checks on job applicants to ensure that nobody with a criminal record is hired.
- Report any employee "high-risk" warning signs to the director of security.
- Carry out high-risk activities (e.g., firing) ensuring that security help is available and notified in advance.
- Abide by personal safety procedures as set up by the director of security.
- Report suspicious persons on premises to security office.

- Research and report on need for personal security devices to be furnished to employees.

Premises Security

- Secure premises when responsible for closing, 100% of the time.
- Maintain lighting system so 95% of lights work at any given time.
- Set alarm system properly at the end of the day, 100% of time.
- Patrol assigned areas on time and in the required manner.

Traffic Control

- Use clear and correct hand signals when directing traffic, to the supervisor's satisfaction.
- Reduce car-pedestrian parking lot accidents to one or none per year.
- Ensure that fire lanes are kept clear at all times.
- Arrange for removing any vehicles that impede fire lane access within 10 minutes of observing them.
- Keep traffic signage visible and in good repair as per supervisor evaluation.

See also: Workplace Health and Safety

Support—Management

Goals in this section can be used with anyone who manages or supervises support staff employees or who has members of support staff as direct reports.

Communication, Supervision, and Training

- Explain work task requirements to reports, in order to reduce error rates to 1%.
- Create and provide job aids for staff.
- Ensure that staff employees work within authority levels on all tasks.
- Conduct training on new technology systems.
- Monitor 3% of incoming calls to provide feedback to employees.
- Advise staff on methods to improve productivity.
- Interpret policy and advise staff on policy interpretations.
- Develop and maintain accurate job descriptions for supervised positions.
- Train new hires in operation of office machines within three days of hire.

Office Management

- Identify alternate sources for office supplies, to reduce costs by 10%.
- Increase throughput by 10% without additional staff.
- Respond to complaints from users about support functions within one working day.
- Reduce days lost due to injuries from ergonomic problems by 8%.
- Draft cost-benefit reports for technological improvements under consideration.

- Negotiate office equipment maintenance contracts to hold costs stable for 20XX.

Scheduling and Work Assignments

- Ensure adequate job coverage of staff absences.
- Schedule staff to reduce overtime to 5% of total hours worked.
- Assign work to staff to make best use of time and skills.
- Accommodate the special needs of staff without sacrificing productivity.

See also: Customer Service and Support—Management, Support

Support

Goals in this section can be used with employees carrying out various support functions—filing, reception, switchboard, and handling phone calls.

Clerical/Filing

- Ensure that there are no more than 10 case files at one time in the "to file" basket.
- Log shared files taken by staff so that others needing the files can locate them.
- Review the filing system once each year to determine efficiency of system.
- Retrieve files within five minutes of file request.
- Ensure that other employees can retrieve files on their own without the help of a clerk.
- Check forms submitted for errors so that no more than 2% of the forms filed contain errors.
- Process forms within three days of receipt.
- Maintain file security and access control so that zero unauthorized accesses occur.
- Ensure that no more than 1% of files are lost or otherwise unavailable.
- Take outgoing mail to mailroom by 4 P.M. each day.

Reception

- Inform all visitors of the approximate wait time, accurate within 10 minutes.
- Greet all visitors within three minutes of arrival.
- Provide staff with enough information about the needs of visitors so they can reduce meeting time.
- Receive no more than one complaint per month about the service provided to visitors.

- Keep reception area clean and orderly.
- Track the availability of employees, in order to provide accurate information to visitors.
- Open the office promptly at 8:00 A.M. 95% of the time.

Secretarial

- Produce outgoing documents with no errors in the final draft.
- Schedule meetings with no conflicts.
- Make travel arrangements to take advantage of advance booking specials.
- Schedule so that all outgoing correspondence is dispatched within one day.
- Prioritize incoming mail and eliminate all unwanted mail to the satisfaction of the manager.
- Edit dictated copy to produce documents that the manager considers better than the text as dictated.
- Summarize and submit travel expense vouchers within three days of the trip.
- Prepare meeting briefing notes for the manager and have them available at least two hours before each meeting.
- Arrange and reserve meeting space and provide refreshments to the satisfaction of the participants.
- Order office supplies so that employees always have materials when they need them.
- Maintain accurate distribution lists for memos.
- Follow up on e-mails sent to ensure they were received and understood.
- Screen e-mails to reduce volume to staff by 50%.
- Fill requests for duplicating within four hours of request.
- Collate and staple documents for professional look, to the satisfaction of the document owner.

Switchboard/Phones

- Prioritize phone calls to the satisfaction of the manager.
- Take messages with sufficient detail to allow informed callbacks.
- Provide sufficient information to callers so return calls can be reduced by 10%.
- Route phone calls to the appropriate person 98% of the time.
- Process a minimum of 20 calls per hour, as needed.
- Answer all calls within three rings.
- Ensure that no caller is kept on hold longer than one minute.
- Screen calls and provide information to caller, to reduce the need for other employees to call back.
- Ensure that phones are covered during breaks, lunch, and short absences.
- Speak clearly so that no more than one complaint is received per month about being hard to understand.

See also: Customer Service and Support, Financial

Transit/Transportation

Goals in this section can be used for employees directly involved in transporting people, including public bus and school bus drivers and taxi and limousine service personnel.

Customer Support

- Handle customer complaints so that the supervisor needs to deal with no more than one complaint a year.
- Provide accurate and courteous information to passengers when they ask.
- Assist elderly passengers into and out of vehicle.
- Receive at least one commendation per year from a passenger.
- Offer to help passengers with their baggage as they enter and exit the vehicle.
- Deliver passengers to airport at the appropriate terminal without loss of time.
- Ensure zero instances of a passenger missing a flight as a result of driver error.
- Arrive at each bus stop on route within two minutes of scheduled time except during weather emergencies.
- Discipline children on school bus in a consistent manner and inform the principal of all disciplinary problems.
- Take every passenger to his or her destination by the most direct or lowest-cost route.

General Operations

- Arrive for each shift ready and able to drive.
- Wear prescribed work clothing and begin shifts with clothing clean and neat.

- Ensure that passengers arrive at their stops on schedule 95% of trips (excluding weather emergencies).
- Follow all tariff rates and procedures 100% of the time.
- Receive zero validated complaint judgments from the taxi board.
- Enforce no smoking laws as required, in polite and courteous fashion.
- Refrain from picking up fares in areas where it is illegal to make pickups.
- Arrive 10 minutes before route to check messages and perform pre-trip inspection.
- Perform a pre-trip under-the-hood and drivetrain inspection daily.
- Ensure that each child boarding bus has a proper and visible identification tag.
- Maintain and submit trip logs to the supervisor at the end of each shift.
- Apply company rules on accepting large-denomination bills.

Safety and Maintenance

- Ensure that the vehicle does not go into service with any mechanical problems that might affect safety.
- Eliminate all passenger injuries caused by preventable mechanical problems.
- Receive no more than one validated complaint about vehicle operation in any calendar year.
- Receive zero tickets for speeding or other traffic violations.
- Receive no more than one validated complaint per year regarding cleanliness of vehicle.
- Maintain safety certification as required by local authority.
- Ensure that all passengers are in compliance with safety requirements before the vehicle moves.

- Inspect any safety exits at the beginning of each shift and report problems immediately.
- Refuse or delay trips when conditions constitute a safety hazard to passengers or equipment.
- Follow safety procedures for dealing with aggressive passengers.
- Complete a defensive driving course once every two years.
- Meet or exceed all physical fitness qualifications required by the company and the licensing authority.
- Remain in or with the bus at all times or otherwise secure access.
- Communicate emergency evacuation procedures to passengers as indicated in the procedures manual.
- Ensure that child passengers are legally and safely in child safety seats before putting vehicle into motion.

Vehicle Operation

- Ensure that no passenger injuries occur as a result of abrupt or extreme driving procedures.
- Drive vehicle to maximize fuel mileage, keeping mileage within 10% of average for vehicle type.
- Activate "No Passing" lights 100% of the time when children are boarding or leaving bus.
- Come to a complete stop at railroad crossings 100% of the time (or as legally required).
- Reduce vehicle repair costs by 10% next year.

See also: Customer Service and Support

Workplace Health and Safety—Management

Goals in this section can be used with managers, supervisors, and team leaders whose reports deal directly with workplace health and safety programs and issues.

Compliance

- Ensure the handling of hazardous material is in compliance with federal regulations.
- Report hazardous material incidents to appropriate government agency within two days of identifying them.
- Ensure that warnings from inspectors are addressed and problems are resolved so that the governing organization takes no further action.
- Reduce government inspection warnings to zero for 20XX.
- Eliminate safety risks that could result in plant shutdowns.

Improvement and Investigation

- Work as a liaison with external investigators to the satisfaction of those investigators.
- Reduce workplace safety insurance fees by 10% in 20XX.
- Reduce accidents requiring hospitalization by 10% per year.
- Reduce minor accidents requiring nurse's station involvement by 15% per year.
- Reduce days lost due to accidents to no more than 1% of total days worked.
- Reduce at-work fatalities to zero by 20XX.
- Reduce the incidence of occupational disease by 15% by 20XX.
- Develop enhanced systems for collecting accident data, to allow the development of concrete accident-reduction strategies.

- Keep and maintain complete, accurate, and timely records of safety violations and incidents.

Training and Communication

- Identify at least three sources for safety-related training and recommend the best option to the COO, based on cost and effectiveness.
- Ensure that 98% of employees are trained in the handling of hazardous materials.
- Ensure that courses receive an average rating of at least 3 out of 5 from participants for the potential of the training to reduce accidents.
- Maintain the no-show rate for training at less than 10% per month.
- Identify and prioritize corporate training requirements based on frequency and severity of accidents.
- Communicate health and safety objectives to all new hires within two weeks of hire.
- Create performance standards regarding safety for each employee supervised.
- Communicate workplace emergency evacuation procedures to all employees at least once every six months.
- Conduct emergency drills at least once every month, with complete compliance to standards (time needed to evaluate, shut down, etc.).
- Track changes in legislation and ensure that the company is in complete compliance within the time frame established by any new legislation.
- Develop and implement employee reward and recognition program for reducing accidents.
- Ensure that all employees can recite emergency phone numbers for various types of incidents.

- Ensure that job aids and safety posters are available and visible in all high-risk areas.

Work Environment

- Develop safe production shutdown procedures so the system can be shut down within five minutes after a safety problem is identified.
- Ensure that all subcontractors and service providers understand and abide by company safety procedures.
- Ensure that equipment maintenance schedules are followed.
- Ensure that the initial response time for treating injured workers is less than 15 minutes for each incident.
- Audit physical space arrangements and make recommendations to ensure staff safety in the event of violent incidents.
- Invite community law enforcement officials once a year to audit workplace procedures for preventing workplace violence.

See also: Security—Management

Workplace Health and Safety

Goals in this section can be used with employees responsible for managing and implementing workplace health and safety programs and issues, work teams with similar responsibilities, and individuals.

Compliance

- Ensure the handling of hazardous material is in compliance with federal regulations.
- Report hazardous material incidents to appropriate government agency within two days of identifying them.
- Maintain your own HAZMAT certification in accordance with government requirements.
- Follow all safety-related guidelines for construction site procedures.
- Ensure that warnings from inspectors are addressed and problems are resolved so that the governing organization takes no further action.
- Reduce government inspection warnings to zero for next year.
- Eliminate safety risks that could result in plant shutdowns.

Improvement and Investigation

- Work as a liaison with external investigators to the satisfaction of those investigators.
- Reduce accidents requiring hospitalization by 10% per year.
- Reduce minor accidents requiring nurse's station involvement by 15% per year.
- Reduce days lost due to accidents to no more than 1% of total days worked.
- Attend and contribute to Workplace Health and Safety Committee meetings, as perceived by other members.

- Reduce at-work fatalities to zero by end of 20XX.
- Reduce the incidence of occupational disease by 15% by 20XX.
- Develop enhanced systems for collecting accident data, to allow the development of concrete accident-reduction strategies.
- Keep and maintain complete, accurate, and timely records of safety violations and incidents.

Training and Communication

- Deliver safety-related training across company so that 90% of employees achieve a minimum of 80% on final course tests.
- Attend and pass defensive driving courses at least once every year.
- Identify at least three sources for safety-related training and recommend the best option to the COO, based on cost and effectiveness.
- Ensure that 98% of employees are trained in the handling of hazardous materials.
- Ensure that courses receive an average rating of at least 3 out of 5 from participants for the potential of the training to reduce accidents.
- Maintain the no-show rate for training at less than 10% per month.
- Identify and prioritize corporate training requirements based on frequency and severity of accidents.
- Communicate health and safety objectives to all new hires within two weeks of hire.
- Create performance standards regarding safety for each employee supervised.
- Communicate workplace emergency evacuation procedures to all employees at least once every six months.

- Conduct emergency drills at least once every month, with complete compliance with standards (time needed to evaluate, shut down, etc.).
- Track changes in legislation and ensure that the company is in complete compliance within the time frame established by any new legislation.
- Develop and implement employee reward and recognition program for reducing accidents.
- Ensure that all employees can recite emergency phone numbers for various types of incidents.
- Ensure that job aids and safety posters are available and visible in all high-risk areas.

Work Environment

- Develop safe production shutdown procedures so the system can be shut down within five minutes after a safety problem is identified.
- Ensure that all subcontractors and service providers understand and abide by company safety procedures.
- Keep all emergency exits repaired and functioning properly at all times.
- Conduct weekly inspections to ensure that all safety equipment is in place and operable.
- Ensure that the initial response time for treating injured workers is less than 15 minutes for each incident.
- Audit physical space arrangements and make recommendations to ensure staff safety in the event of violent incidents.
- Invite community law enforcement officials once a year to audit workplace procedures for preventing workplace violence.

See also: Security

About the Author

Robert Bacal is an accomplished consultant, book author, trainer, and public speaker. He is the author of *Perfect Phrases for Performance Reviews* (with Douglas Max), *Perfect Phrases for Managing Your Small Business* (with Nancy Moore), *Perfect Phrases for Customer Service*, *Manager's Guide to Performance Reviews*, *Managing Performance*, and several other books. He is an active management consultant and popular speaker. His website, **www.work911.com**, includes many articles and other materials to help managers and employees improve performance in all aspects of their jobs.

The Right Phrase for Every Situation...Every Time

THE IDEAL PERFORMANCE SUPPORT SOLUTION FOR MANAGERS AND SUPERVISORS

With over 30,000 phrases, *Perfect Phrases for Managers* is an unmatched digital resource that provides managers at every level with the skills they need to effectively manage any situation.

From performance reviews to documenting problems, to motivating and coaching teams, to managing difficult people and embarrassing situations, this performance support tool will help your company create an environment for exceptional performance.

Go to **www.perfectphrases.com** to learn more about *Perfect Phrases for Managers* and how you can access:

- A "Things to Consider" section with hundreds of bite-size coaching tips
- Audio clips from actual conversations
- Strategies for opening up healthy communication

The right phrase for every situation, every time.

Visit www.perfectphrases.com to learn how your company can qualify for a trial subscription.